MUSIC

for the man who enjoys
Hamlet

Also by B. H. HAGGIN

B. H. HAGGIN has been writing on music since 1923. He was music critic of the Brooklyn *Daily Eagle* from 1934 to 1937; in 1936 he became records critic and from 1939 to 1957 he was music critic of the *Nation;* from 1946 to 1949 he wrote a column, "Music on the Radio," for the Sunday New York *Herald Tribune;* and he now reviews records in the *New Republic* and the *Yale Review* and other musical events in the *Hudson Review.* His other books are *A Book of the Symphony* (1937), *Music on Records* (1938 and 1941), *Music in the Nation* (1949), *The Listener's Musical Companion* (1956) and *Conversations with Toscanini* (1959).

MUSIC
for the man who enjoys
Hamlet

by

B. H. HAGGIN

VINTAGE BOOKS

A DIVISION OF RANDOM HOUSE

New York

CONTENTS

FOREWORD

ALTHOUGH ostensibly this book is addressed to the musically inexperienced reader, actually it is written for the musically experienced reader as well. Addressing the inexperienced reader permits me to begin with material which is intended to be enlightening and helpful to him in his approach to music, but which I also consider worth the experienced reader's attention; and in these introductory pages I cite pieces of music which I judge to be immediately accessible and impressive to the inexperienced ear, but which are among those most valued by experienced listeners. And it is with such music that the book is concerned after the introductory pages.

The musically untrained reader should not be frightened away by the passages in musical notation. This is a book intended to be read *as one listens*—with the words charting a course through what one hears, and with the passages in musical notation helping the mind to grasp important details by having the eye follow what the ear is taking in. The reader will do best to familiarize himself with the sound of the quoted passages by playing them, or having someone else play them, on the piano before he listens to the piece played on a record.

Certain of the pieces of music are presented in complete detail—after which others require and are given less detailed treatment.

"But this much I do affirm, and shall be ready to Prove, by Demonstration, (to any Person Intelligible) That Musick is as a Language, and has Its Significations, as Words have, (if not more strongly) only most people do not understand that Language, (perfectly)."

THOMAS MACE: *"Musick's Monument; or a Remembrancer of the Best Practical Musick, both Divine and Civil, that has ever been known to have been in the World"* (1676).

Music for the Man Who Enjoys 'Hamlet'

YOU reach home, let us say, with expectations of a quiet dinner, of slippers, easy chair, a much read copy of *Hamlet* to take your mind far from the wearying details and arguments and vexations of the long day at the office. And you learn with dismay that this is the night of the third concert of the city's major series, that your wife is going, and you are going with her.

"*Schnabel* is playing!"—and it is evident that your eyes should light up in anticipation; but instead you groan in recollection. Later, after a hurried change of clothes, a rushed dinner, seated uncomfortably beside your wife in the concert hall while a gray-haired man plays something called Sonata in B flat major by Schubert, you think, as you fold and unfold your program: "It seems to mean a lot to Schnabel, and I suppose it means something to all these other people; but it doesn't make sense to me." But by the time Schnabel is playing Beethoven's Sonata Opus 111 your boredom has given way to irritation; and savagely throwing away the shreds of your program you think: "I'll bet it doesn't mean any more to the others or to the old boy on the stage than it means to me. It *doesn't* make sense; and they're only pretending it does."

Some of them may be pretending; but the music Schnabel is playing does make sense—to him, and to others; it makes as much sense, and the same kind of sense, as *Hamlet* makes to you. You don't see that; but you will, I think, if we consider what *Hamlet* is and what it does.

To begin with, *Hamlet* is an example of the employment, on a very large scale, of an artistic medium. The nature of this employment we may see more easily in a small-scale example—one of the Sonnets:

Full many a glorious morning have I seen
Flatter the mountain-tops with sovereign eye,
Kissing with golden face the meadows green,
Gilding pale streams with heavenly alchymy;
Anon permit the basest clouds to ride
With ugly rack on his celestial face,
And from the forlorn world his visage hide,
Stealing unseen to west with this disgrace:
Even so my sun one early morn did shine,
With all-triumphant splendour on my brow;
But, out! alack! he was but one hour mine,
The region cloud hath mask'd him from me now.
    Yet him for this my love no whit disdaineth;
    Suns of the world may stain when heaven's sun staineth.

Other men have had thoughts and emotions about the love they have possessed and lost; what they have not done is to elaborate these thoughts and emotions into the complex form of words, rich in rhythmed sound, in images, in overtones of sense and feeling, in which Shakespeare makes *his* thoughts and emotions on the subject articulate. The articulateness in words in metrical patterns is common enough: it produces huge quantities of worthless poetry by children, adolescents, adults. In Shakespeare's sonnet, however,

2

the quality of the mere articulateness in the medium is itself uncommon; and its complexities and splendors represent in addition the workings of an uncommonly complex and rich mind and personality. Involved, that is, with the articulateness, operating through it, crystallized in the completed poem, are Shakespeare's personal resources—what he is in character, mind, feeling, what he has lived through, what his experience has done to him, what insights it has given him. This is true even of the sonnet; and it is true more obviously, more richly, more excitingly, of *Hamlet*.

If you are moved, excited, exalted by *Hamlet*, if for a time afterwards the real world appears to you wonderfully changed, that is because for several hours you have been looking through Shakespeare's eyes at an imagined world created between the covers of a book or on the stage of a theater—a world in which the natures of the human beings who inhabit it, the situations in which they are placed, the things they do and say all express significances which life has come to have for this man with perceptions and insights that you and I do not possess. If *Hamlet* leaves you with an impression of greatness, that impression is one of the greatness of mind and spirit which Shakespeare reveals in his play. And if the insights of that mind and spirit impress you as much as they do, that is because of the richness of the poetic form in which they are embodied and presented to you.

Which brings us to this important fact: that if you are affected by *Hamlet*, it is first of all because you have the personal resources which enable you to appreciate the insights it conveys; but it is also—and this is the important thing for our discussion—because you have the susceptibility to the poetic medium that enables you to be affected by the poetic form in which these insights are conveyed. I say this is the important thing for our discussion because similar insights are conveyed in Schubert's B flat Sonata and Beethoven's Opus 111, but through a different artistic medium: if they do not get through to your mind, it is because the *medium* is one to which, at the moment, you are not susceptible.

"Perhaps even Shakespeare never reached that final state of illumination that is expressed in some of Beethoven's late music," says Sullivan in his excellent book about Beethoven. If the state of illumination that is conveyed to you by Shakespeare is not conveyed by Beethoven in his second movement of the Sonata Opus 111, the reason is that you are susceptible to Shakespeare's medium of artistic communication but not to Beethoven's; and you will understand how this might be so, if you consider how long and how much you have read and seen Shakespeare, who uses the words that are your own medium of communication and expression, and how few encounters you have had with Beethoven, whose musical idiom is not that of the folk-songs or school-songs or Broadway show-songs you may be familiar with.

Understanding this, you may be disposed to try an experiment—which is to listen to the opening passage of that movement of Opus 111 at least once every evening for a couple of weeks, in order to become thoroughly familiar with it, and to see whether, as you come to know it, you begin to get from it some communication of what a man like Beethoven might feel at the end of his life—the sense of experience mastered, of profound lessons learned, of resignation, inner illumination achieved. Here is the passage (and for the present resist the temptation to listen beyond it):

Adagio molto semplice [e] cantabile
[slowly, very simply, in singing style]

In this passage the uppermost notes are the 'melody', through which the meaning of the musical statement is largely conveyed; each group of notes below a note of the melody is a 'chord' in the 'harmony' that enriches this meaning.

You will be serving the purpose of the experiment and increasing its chances of success if you listen in the same way to another passage—the opening statement in the first movement of Schubert's Sonata in B flat, which in a different way also communicates the sense of profound lessons learned, inner illumination achieved:

And listen to two other passages for what they may communicate to you. One is the beginning of the third movement of Beethoven's Trio Opus 97—the two statements of the piano that are echoed by the violin and cello:

The other is the statement of the piano with which the first movement of Beethoven's Piano Concerto No. 4 begins:

I have suggested a couple of weeks; but obviously the experiment doesn't have to stop after two weeks. Give yourself all the time you may need to find those passages of music acquiring significance for you, or on the other hand to satisfy yourself that music is not for you the medium of artistic communication which you are willing to believe it is for others.

I F now those passages do convey significance to you, we can go on—first of all to get a more precise idea of this significance and how it is conveyed.

In the sonnet I quoted, or in one of Hamlet's soliloquies, we see a complex form of words embody and communicate a complex synthesis of thought and emotion. And if anyone were to ask "What thought, what emotion?", the answer would be "The thought and emotion expressed and defined by that form of words." One can say that the sonnet is concerned with the love which is given and then withheld; one can say further that this love is compared with the sun which lights the earth and then is hidden by clouds; but to do this is not to convey the rich overtones of sense and feeling that are expressed by

> Full many a glorious morning have I seen
> Flatter the mountain-tops with sovereign eye,
> Kissing with golden face the meadows green,
> Gilding pale streams with heavenly alchymy;

and the rest of the poem. The only way of conveying those overtones is to state the precise form of words that Shakespeare himself devised for this purpose.

A painter too may be aware only of choosing a bit of paint and placing it on the canvas in relation to a number of other bits; but the choice, the placing, the relation involve exercise of judgment—which is to say that they involve the whole man, the sum at that moment of his experience, thought, emotion, insight. What is involved in the choices and uses of the bits of paint reveals itself through them; and in the end the completed integrated arrangement of lines, colors, planes, masses and forms is a visual embodiment and communication of a particular synthesis of that experience, thought, emotion, insight.

Roger Fry has described the process of a Cézanne, still-life, in which the bottles, pears and apples, so commonplace as to have no emotional associations in themselves, are "deprived of all those specific characters by which we ordinarily apprehend their concrete existence," and are "reduced to pure elements of space and volume" which are then "coordinated and organized by the artist's sensual intelligence." He refers to Cézanne's own conception that it was out of

8

these relations of formal elements that emotion was
to emanate; and he says: "One may wonder whether
painting has ever aroused graver, more powerful,
more massive emotions than those to which we are
compelled by some of Cézanne's masterpieces in this
genre." And these emotions to which we are compelled—not by the subjects of the paintings, but by
the pictorial treatment of the subjects—these grave,
powerful, massive emotions are something we have
no way of knowing or defining or conveying, other
than by those relations of formal elements on the
canvas that were Cézanne's way.

And so with the piece of music that is a formal
organization of sound—or sounds—in time. The sounds
have no external references to objects or ideas; what
they have is the internal coherence of a kind of
grammar of their own; the relations in which they are
placed—in a texture of horizontal lines of sounds in
sequence (melody) and vertical lines of sounds in
simultaneous combination (harmony), articulated by
duration and stress (rhythm), and colored by the
timbres of instruments or voices—are governed basi-
cally by this grammar, which is used in an individual
style by each composer, in obedience to the laws of
his own being. He too, that is, may be aware only of
choosing a sound and placing it in relation to a number of others; but the choice, the placing, the relation,
involving exercise of judgment as they do, involve the
sum at that moment of his experience, thought, emotion, insight—of which a particular synthesis is finally
embodied and communicated in the completed formal
arrangement of sounds. If anyone were to ask about
the second movement of Beethoven's Sonata Opus 111
"What thought, what emotion, what insight?", one

9

could say, as I did earlier, "The sense of experience mastered, lessons learned, resignation, inner illumination achieved." But one would have to use the same words about the opening of Schubert's B flat Sonata, to describe experience mastered, lessons learned, resignation and illumination achieved that are different from Beethoven's and expressed in different musical terms. This demonstrates the inadequacy of the words, and the fact that here again we have no way of knowing or defining or conveying the particular synthesis of experience and emotion that is embodied in each piece of music, other than by the formal construction in sound that each man used for the purpose.

One might, for that matter, find no other words than "experience mastered, lessons learned, resignation and illumination achieved" for other pieces of music by Beethoven himself—that is, for the same synthesis of experience and emotion that embodies itself in different constructions of sound. From this we realize that in dealing with a work of art we are concerned not with meaning but with meaning as embodied in form. We read Shakespeare not merely for his profound insights, but for these insights as made explicit and affecting in his rich poetic forms; and so with Cézanne's powerful emotions, and the inner illumination and exaltation of Beethoven in his last years. We are, then, interested in each different formal construction on canvas from which we get the impact of the same powerful emotions, each different construction of sound which conveys to us the same inner illumination and exaltation.

I have gone into all this to get you to see that just as the way to understand Shakespeare's poem is to read it, and the way to understand Cézanne's still-life is to look at it, so the way—the only way—to understand Beethoven's or Schubert's sonata movement is the one you have already used successfully with its opening passage—to listen to it. It was natural for you, when the music made no sense, to ask to be told what its sense was, and to ask to be told in words, since you were accustomed to think of sense as expressible in words. And it was necessary for you to learn to apprehend from a phrase of music a sense which was not definable by words—which was defined solely by the particular organization of sounds in that phrase of music. You may say that I did use words to describe it and help you apprehend it; but they did not really describe what in the end you had to apprehend from the music and would have apprehended even without my words; and you will discover, when you are accustomed to the medium, that the meaning of a phrase of Beethoven or Schubert is grasped with the sounds, immediately, and usually without difficulty. If there is any difficulty, what is needed is not explanation of the phrase in words but repeated hearing of it. And you cannot get a wrong idea by listening to Beethoven or Schubert himself, but you will get some very wrong ideas by listening to the people who undertake to speak for him.

It was natural for you also, when the music made no sense, to think that you might understand it if you were told things about it—about the man who wrote it, the period in which he lived, the ideas, tendencies, forces which influenced him. But when you have experienced the joyousness, buoyancy and exuberant playfulness embodied in Beethoven's Eighth Symphony you may be surprised to discover the vexations and turmoil that filled his daily life at the time he was writing this work; and you will learn from this that the biographical and historical background of a work of art may be quite irrelevant to it. For it is the inner core of personal qualities, emotions and insights created by a lifetime of experience that governs the artist's selection and arrangement of words or paints or sounds in a poem or picture or symphony; and although this inner core is constantly altered and developed by his continuing experience, it is not affected by any and every happening of the day. When this inner development in Beethoven had reached the emotions and attitudes we are made aware of by the Eighth Symphony, they pressed for expression in the sounds of this symphony, unaffected by the external turmoil that was irrelevant to them. Earlier too it was the heroic emotions and attitudes that Beethoven had developed in the face of disaster, which operated through his articulateness in his medium to produce the *Eroica* Symphony; if there had been no French Revolution there would have been no dedication to Napoleon to tear up when he made himself emperor, but there would have been the same *Eroica* Symphony. And Ernest Newman once pointed to the striking differences in the three great symphonies that Mozart wrote in those two months of wretchedness and despair in the summer of 1788, as evidence of the fact that "the creative imagination of a great artist functions too deep down within him to be greatly affected by anything that may happen on the surface of his life or his being. The subconscious is of much more importance in the artist than the conscious; and the subconscious proceeds by its own mysterious inner chemistry and obeys its own mysterious laws." It is, then, not the biographical or historical background that gives us a clue to the meaning of the music; it is rather the music that often gives us our only clue to what was going on inside the composer.

But to know even relevant biographical and historical details *about* a work of art would not make the relations of elements *in* the work of art clearer and more significant. It is true, as we have seen, that the whole man was involved in the process which produced the Cézanne still-life; and it is further true that with the man there must have been involved, more remotely, the influences which had operated on him— the general ideas, the social and political conditions of the time. But when you knew these things that were involved in the process you would still have to perceive and feel the impact of the formal relations of space and volume that are the result of the process; and for this the things you knew about Cézanne's life would be neither necessary nor helpful. And so with Beethoven's or Schubert's sonata.

Nor do you need the technical knowlege of the professional musician. A piece of music is, to begin with, an organization of sounds; experiencing it begins with hearing the sounds and the way they are related in each phrase, the relation of one phrase to the next in the progression; and learning to hear these relations is at the same time a process by which you learn to follow the grammar and logic of musical thought, the operations by which it proceeds; but you can do all this without knowing the technical facts and names of what you are hearing. For one of those opening passages to acquire significance for you it was necessary to hear the sounds and their relations, for which you did not have to know that the tonic of C major was followed by a second inversion of the dominant seventh—any more than you have to know that a particular brown which you see in a painting is called burnt umber, and another which is placed in relation to it is called yellow ochre. What is true is that when you have heard something you will find the name of it convenient to use in referring to it; and I certainly will find the name convenient to use when I refer to it in talking to you. But a great many matters which the professional is concerned with, and the terms which he uses in discussing them—these you don't have to know anything about.

And now let us get on with what comes after the opening passage—you listening, and I pointing out what there is for you to hear.

W HEN you look at a painting you get a first visual impression of the entire formal design, and a first emotional impact from this impression; then, as your eye moves about on the canvas taking in the detail, the impression and effect on you become elaborated and complex. And your eye is free to move in any direction, to take in the details in any order, to do this slowly or quickly. In a piece of music, on the other hand, the formal design is not revealed all at once, but only bit by bit in an order and at a rate determined, for his purpose, by the composer. When, therefore, you listen to the first statement in the second movement of Beethoven's Sonata Opus 111:

you get your first aural impression and emotional impact from the first coherent group of sounds, [a]; this impression and its effect are elaborated somewhat by the next group, [b]; the elaborated impression and effect are elaborated further by [c], and the newly elaborated impression and effect by [d]. Further elaboration and complexity come with the repetition of the entire statement [1], then with each additional detail of the answering statement [2]:

then with the repetition of this answer.

What you have heard up to this point is the 'theme' of the movement; and in the remainder of the movement further elaboration of aural impression and emotional effect results from what is done with this theme.

Listen to it again; and then listen to the passage which follows immediately after it: note that what you are hearing is at once similar to the theme and different from it. As you listen let your eye follow the contours of the musical notation—first of the theme, then of its new and different statement:

Note first that in the new statement the melody progresses in terms of the figure [x]; note further that this figuration weaves about the sounds of the theme marked with asterisks—these sounds, then, being what makes the new statement sound similar to the theme, while the weaving about them makes it sound different; and note also that with this elaboration of contour there is elaboration of the significance conveyed by the theme.

This new statement is an example of the 'variation process' in music; and it is by this process that the movement continues, building up its structure and its impact. If you interrupt to ask me the question you may feel impelled to ask—*why* Beethoven elaborates the theme with this particular figuration, I can only remind you of what I said in the preceding section, and answer that what he does proceeds from the deep necessities like those which lead a painter to choose a bit of yellow ochre after a bit of burnt umber: they make it the right thing for him to do—the right means, for the right effect.

Music for the man who enjoys Hamlet

Each of the two parts of the theme is varied; and each part of the variation—like each part of the theme —is repeated. In Variation 2 the figuration is faster, more intricate, with increased intensity in the effect:

In Variation 3 the figuration is still faster and more intricate, and suddenly impassioned and violent:

And now suddenly the violence subsides into the hush and mystery of Variation 4, with its blocking

out of the essentials of the theme in soft chords above
a softly vibrating bass:

This time, instead of the usual repetition of the first
part you hear a further variation: from the hush and
mystery you are suddenly swept up to clear, daz-
zling radiance at ethereal heights—to rapid figuration,
heard as though at a distance, in the higher tonal
region:

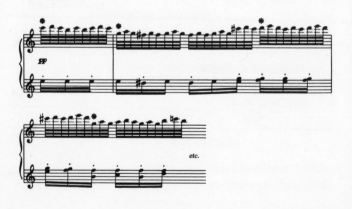

Part 2 follows—first the soft chords over vibrating bass, then the rapid figuration high up and far away. The two variations on each part of the theme, instead of one variation repeated, make No. 4 a 'double variation'.

This leads now to a long digression—a freely-moving section, in which you are made aware of ever increasing involvement and ever wider-ranging emotional implications. That is, when Variation 4 ends, the rapid figuration of Variation 4 continues, descending, coming nearer; it leads to a passage:

which, in its increasing urgency, makes you aware that it is heading for something important: a 'trill' (a rapid alternation of two adjacent sounds), with [1a] of the theme hammered out down below, then echoed up above:

The trill continues, more softly; you are aware of a shift to a new tonal region:

[1b]

there is a swelling of trills; then one trill climbs higher and higher; and suddenly the bass strikes in with violence, creating a tension which is released in a somewhat elaborated statement, in a new tonal region, of [1d] of the theme:

The last two measures are 'developed'—which is to say that the same melodic contour is produced at successively different heights in the tonal medium, by different sounds, with differences in the meaning conveyed. The development creates increasing involvement; and suddenly you are brought out of all this involvement into the clear—out of the long digression back to the theme itself, stated this time over excitingly fast-moving and enriching figuration:

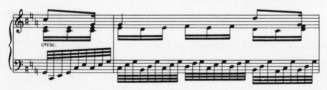

This figuration imparts a new and gradually increasing intensity and splendor to the theme, which in this way works up from a quiet beginning to a joyous, an ecstatic proclamation of inner exaltation. The conclusion of the theme is developed; and the development pushes the jubilant exaltation to a higher and higher point, and finally to a trill, which, with the vibration in a lower voice, creates a tonal radiance for the ethereal statement of the theme:

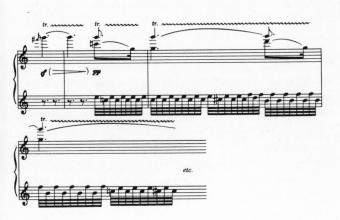

and then for fragmentary echoes of the theme; after which the trill dissolves into rapid figuration that climbs high to descend to last forceful statements of

[1a] of the theme, which build up a momentary tension that is resolved in quiet concluding chords: the end is still inner exaltation, and peace.

If your powers of perception and retention were more than human you would have been able to hear all these details and formal relations between details the very first time you listened to the movement straight through—which is the way it was meant to be listened to. Since your powers are only human, listening in this way you would have missed a great deal which you would have picked up at later hearings. That, in fact, is the way you will get to know much of the music you will encounter, and some of the music we shall consider in this book. But in some instances you will do what we have done with the movement of Beethoven's Opus 111; and now, after this attention to detail after detail, section after section, listen to the movement straight through from beginning to end, hearing the form in sound revealed in time as a continuous progression, and receiving from it the cumulative effect and impact it was intended to produce. Do this once, twice, or as many times as you need for the movement to become something grasped and assimilated as an entity. Then put it aside while you go on with the other music we are to consider in this book, and go back to it after a week; put it aside again, and go back to it after a longer interval; and continue to hear it only at intervals. At each such rehearing it will strike you with fresh impact, and with richer, greater meaning.

THE detailed presentation of this piece of music has been intended, first of all, to bring it within the range of your experience and understanding; and I should add that the only thing

22

I consider important about an art is the particular
and unique work of art as something to be experienced and understood, and the only thing I wish to
achieve in this book is your experience and understanding of particular and unique pieces of music.
The presentation of the movement from Beethoven's
sonata also has acquainted you with one of the
processes of the musical medium, the variation process, and with the variation form; and this knowledge
will make it easier for you to grasp the detail and
formal outline of other pieces of music which use
the same process and form.

You will find another great example by Beethoven
in the last movement of his Piano Sonata Opus 109
(when the Victor recording of Schnabel's performance
is issued). It begins with a theme no less sublime
and affecting than that of the variation movement of
Opus 111; it ends no less wonderfully in its own way,
the last variation proceeds with ever increasing momentum and intensity achieved through increasingly
rapid figuration that culminates, at the climax, in
trills; and the climax and trills die out into a simple
restatement of the original theme, which is—after the
involvements that have intervened—even more sublime and affecting than its first statement. (This
effect, in music, of the return to something which has
been departed from is one to take note of. We have
already encountered it in the movement of Opus 111—
in the richly elaborated restatement of the theme
after the long digression; and we shall encounter it
many times again.) And long after you have finished
with all the music we shall deal with in this book
you might tackle the great structure that Beethoven
erects on the basis of an absurd little waltz-tune by
Diabelli, with those slow variations—Nos. 20, 29, 30,

31—and transitional chords after Variation 32 that take us to the remotest points which Beethoven's mind reached on the "strange seas of thought" of his last works.

Right now, however, we shall consider the third movement of his Trio Opus 97, of which you already know the great opening passage. This passage is the theme—each of its two parts stated first by the piano, then by the violin and cello—for a series of double variations which employ different combinations of timbres and figurations of the three instruments. Thus, the implications of the theme are elaborated and enriched in Variation 1:

which translates the theme into exquisite figuration of the piano against eloquent sustained tones first of the cello, then of the cello and violin.

In Variation 2:

the implications become less grave: the theme is translated into graceful figuration which is tossed be-

tween cello and violin over light accompanying
chords of the piano.

In Variation 3:

there is dramatic urgency in the rumbling thunder of
the piano that builds up a crescendo of intensity, with
comments from violin and cello.

In Variation 4:

you hear the richest textures of sound, with the piano
playing a syncopated melody over unquiet figuration
in the bass, while the violin plays a more tranquil
variation over sustained tones of the cello. And after
this richness you hear the simplicity and quiet of the
beginning of a long section which brings new, wide-
ranging and profound implications. The piano begins
what appears at first to be a restatement of the first
part of the original theme:

but the cello and then the violin intervene to carry
the statement further—after which the piano carries
it to its conclusion; and in the portions played by the
strings there are (at the points marked with asterisks)
changes in the melody, with corresponding changes
in the underlying harmony, which convey the first
of the new implications. The changes are more extensive in the second part—the dialogue of piano and
cello shifting into a new tonal region as it expands
both the form and the new implications; and this ex-
pansion continues: out of the conclusion grows a
wonderful section of increasing involvement, then of

great conclusions (with an additional chord of transition to the last movement of the trio, which we postpone for the moment).

B RAHMS'S Variations on a Theme of Haydn, which we consider now, is a work not of profound implications but of very engaging ones. The theme has been pronounced, with sufficient justification, one of the most beautiful melodies ever written; the variations are a series of charming pieces with only slight apparent connection with the theme; and whereas Beethoven's Trio used combinations of the timbres and figurations of three instruments, Brahms's work uses the greater variety provided by an orchestra constituted as follows:

Woodwinds	*Brass*	*Strings*
Piccolo	4 Horns	First Violins
2 Flutes	2 Trumpets	Second Violins
2 Oboes		Violas
2 Clarinets	*Percussion*	Cellos
2 Bassoons	Kettledrums	Basses
Contrabassoon	Triangle	

In the Theme it is the oboe that you hear on top playing the melody:

with plucked cellos and basses down below; with horns, bassoons and contrabassoon filling in softly at the beginning, and all the remaining woodwinds and brass coming in brilliantly at the end; but with violins and violas silent throughout.

At the beginning of Variation 1 there are ominously reiterated sounds from horns, bassoons, contrabassoon and kettledrum, over which violins play an ascending melody, violas and cellos a descending countermelody; then the increasingly insistent reiterated notes are transferred to piccolo, flutes, oboes and horns, the ascending melody to cellos and bassoons, the descending countermelody to violins and violas (see reproduction of score on page 29).

At the beginning of Variation 2, after the initial explosion of the full orchestra the agitated clarinets are heard on top with a countermelody from violins and violas:

with bassoons doubling the clarinets an octave lower, and with plucked cellos and basses down below.

In Part 1 of Variation 3 oboe and bassoon play the wistful melody over low strings; in the repetition of Part 1 first violins and violas play this melody while flute and bassoon wreathe it in delicate ornamental figures. At the beginning of Part 2 there is this antiphonal passage:

with other instruments contributing the other strands of a rich aural texture; in the repetition of Part 2 the dialogue at the beginning is between oboe and horn, with violas and cellos carrying on a parallel dialogue down below.

In Part 1 of Variation 4 oboe and horn begin the plaintive melody, joined later by flute and bassoon, while a descending countermelody is played by violas and cellos; in the repetition of Part 1 strings have the melody, with the countermelody played by flute and clarinet, joined later by bassoon. In Part 2 the melody of oboe and horn is accompanied and answered by strings; in the repetition of Part 2 the melody of strings is accompanied and answered by woodwinds.

At the beginning of brilliantly mercurial Variation 5 there is the chatter of woodwinds.

At the beginning of Variation 6 a weighty passage for horns is followed by a lighter one for woodwinds.

Variation 7 combines two wistful melodies:

with other instruments contributing the other strands of a rich aural texture.

And in Variation 8 there is the dramatic hush of muted strings, then woodwinds.

Variation 1 of Brahms's Variations on a Theme of Haydn

This brings us to the concluding section of the work—a new series of variations on a new theme, with new and special features in the process that produce a new and special effect. The theme is very brief; it is repeated over and over again as a so-called 'ground-bass' for ever new accompanying phrases; these variations make the repetitions interesting, and produce a cumulative effect by their varied succession; but the special effect of this concluding section is the long crescendo of intensity and the cumulative impact built up by the constant, inexorable repetition of the brief ground-bass.

This is a grave five-measure phrase:

Derived from the first measures of Haydn's melody.

which for a time continues to be played by cellos and basses. Its first statement is accompanied by a texture from the other strings; with the second statement the texture is enriched by horns and woodwinds; with the third there is a melody from violins joined by woodwinds; in the fourth variation this melody is amplified with increasing sonority.

The gradual crescendo in these first four variations leads to a series of four variations that are increasingly vigorous and brilliant.

The vigor and brilliance subside for a series of five variations in which the ground-bass is stated more and more lightly and the accompanying textures are thinned out: first a melody from the violins, then a variation on this melody from the oboe, then this variation played by the other woodwinds, then a new

31

variation on the meldoy from the flute over the ground-bass from horn and lightly plucked violas and cellos, then this new variation played by the other woodwinds, while the ground-bass itself is varied as follows:

Now a series of three variations in which the ground-bass is lifted into prominence: first by oboes, then by flutes, oboes and horns, then by violins and horns—with growing intensity achieved through enriched color and figuration and increased sonority.

And then a sudden hush, with references to Haydn's original melody that blaze up into the full orchestra's joyously brilliant restatement of this melody. In addition to the cumulative impact, then, there is the effect I have pointed out before—the effect of a return, after a long interval, to something that was departed from.

FROM the concluding section of this work of Brahms we go to a series of variations on a ground-bass which builds up to a magnificently powerful construction in sound, with profound and great implications: Bach's *Passacaglia* for organ.

These profound implications begin to be heard at once in the gravely meditative eight-measure ground-bass:

They acquire poignancy from the figure that is developed over the ground-bass in the first and second
variations; and from the strands of melody worked
into the rich texture of the next variation:

theme marked by asterisks

*Melodic lines progressing together in such a texture constitute
'counterpoint'; and the texture is 'contrapuntal'.*

The implications of the ground-bass acquire growing intensity in the following variation from the intricate contrapuntal texture of animated figuration;
in the next the intensity subsides momentarily in a
somewhat playful figuration which is carried into the
ground-bass itself:

(simplified)

The crescendo of intensity is resumed in the next
three variations, in which the ground-bass is heard
with increasingly rich contrapuntal textures; then
comes a quiet variation, with tensions created in the
texture by figuration that again is carried into the
ground-bass:

The tensions in this variation increase, leading to a forceful variation in which the ground-bass is heard with a flowing accompaniment.

Now a quiet and affecting statement of the ground-bass in an upper voice, with a flowing accompaniment in a single voice down below; then another such statement of the ground-bass, acquiring greater urgency from the entrance of additional voices in the flowing accompaniment down below. And then an interlude of three quiet variations: the first wonderfully poignant in implications, with the ground-bass itself varied and obscured in the exquisitely wrought texture:

the second with gracefully flowing figuration that is carried into the ground-bass:

the third hushed and a little mysterious, with the ground-bass itself varied:

The hush is broken by a statement of the ground-bass that acquires explosive force from its accompanying figuration; then comes a statement that is made imposing by a brilliant flowing accompaniment. And then, finally, a series of three variations in which the implications of the ground-bass acquire increasing intensity from increasingly rich accompanying figuration, and attain tremendous concluding force at the end.

But the final chord of the *Passacaglia* is at the same time the beginning of a new piece of musical construction, in a new form which produces its effect by a new process. This is a 'fugue', a contrapuntal form in which a melodic idea, called the 'subject', is discussed in a specified number of melodic lines of thought, or 'voices', that proceed simultaneously.

In the present work the discussion is carried on in four voices; and the first thing that happens is an 'exposition' in which each of the four in turn states the subject—the first half of the ground-bass of the *Passacaglia*:

The subject is heard each time with the countersubject that is printed in small notes; and as each voice finishes the subject it continues with the 'countersubject', while the voice that had the countersubject continues with a second countersubject. Here is the way the exposition works out:

Note the so-called 'episode' that intervenes after the second statement of the subject to delay and give more effect to the third; and the increased intensity as the third and fourth voices enter the discussion and increase the density of the contrapuntal texture.

From this point you hear further statements of the subject, now in one voice, now in another—each such statement leading into an episode, which in turn leads back into the subject; and you hear alternate thinning and thickening of the contrapuntal texture, with alternately decreased and increased intensity. The episodes are successively longer and weightier, making the cumulative impact of each successive return of the subject even greater; and the final statement of the subject has the force of a tremendous peroration.

LET us now go back to another of the passages with which you familiarized yourself earlier in the book—the one from Schubert's Sonata in B flat. It too is the beginning of a spacious construction in sound—a beginning with implications of great meaning that are elaborated into a wide-ranging content as the construction is built up in time. But this time the building procedure is not varied repetition of the single initial passage; instead there are a number of thematic ideas, and these are used and organized in a different way to produce a different effect. The effect is the one we have encountered before—that of the return, after an interval, to what was departed from; but it is magnified this time by the large scale of the cycle of statement, departure and restatement.

As you begin to follow the course of the movement from its opening sentence:

note the faint rumble in the bass like distant thunder, which punctuates its conclusion. After a pause the sentence begins again and continues as before until the point marked with an asterisk, where it changes in a way that gives the implications a new direction and carries them to a new conclusion:

This too is punctuated by the faint rumble in the bass, which falls away into the accompanying figuration of an altered statement of [1], in a new tonal region around the chord marked with asterisks as a center:

The statement carries the implications of [1] in a new direction, and leads into a passage of figuration:

This is an interlude which leads back to an impressively forceful restatement of [2], which now continues beyond its original conclusion, with premonitory shifts in harmony that lead to a new train of thought in a new tonal region around the first chord as a center:

[5] is developed, with the melody transferred to the right hand, and with details in the changing phraseology that are exquisite in sound and poignant in effect. Its conclusion is followed by this passage:

which, after a time, subsides into a wonderful section of retrospective meditation and summation, beginning as follows:

This completes the extensive statement that is the first part of the cycle.

The departure from this statement, and the second part of the cycle, begins with further manipulation of the material you have heard, which develops its implications further: first a new development of [1]; then a new development of [6]. This falls away into an impressive new idea:

which gradually works up to a shattering climax.

The climax breaks off for a poignant development of [8] in a new tonal region around the first chord as center:

Note the sound and effect created by the left hand at the points marked by asterisks.

It is echoed down below; and suddenly you hear the faint rumble of thunder in the bass which you have not heard since the beginning of the movement, and which now introduces a deeply affecting reference to [1]:

Again the rumble of thunder, introducing another reference to [1], with changed implications from its shift in tonal position to the region around the chord marked with an asterisk as center:

41

Again the rumble of thunder, shifting back to [10]:

with the changed harmonies marked with asterisks creating new implications that are carried further as the passage continues. It falls away into silence.

Again the rumble of thunder; then what has been foreshadowed happens: [1] begins again as it began originally—the more affecting for all that has intervened, and starting in this way the restatement of the material of the first part of the cycle. In due time it reaches the section of retrospective meditation and summation—also the more wonderful the second time after all that has intervened. The summation is carried further this time to a new conclusion, which leads to last references . to [1], a last rumble of thunder, and quiet concluding chords.

In the cycle you have just heard the three parts are called—with rare logic for musical terminology—the 'exposition', the 'development', and the 'recapitulation'. And this three-part cycle, in which the middle part develops further some of the material of the first part, is normally the prescribed structure of the first movement of the classical sonata; hence it is sometimes referred to as 'first-movement form'; but also, and more often, as 'sonata form', or as 'sonata-allegro form' because the first movement is normally in quick tempo for which the Italian direction *Allegro* is often used. And here you encounter some of the confusions of musical terminology; for sonata form, it turns out, is not the form of the entire sonata but only the normally prescribed form of its first movement; and it is used also in other movements than the first—sometimes in the second, which is normally slow.

A word also about the shifts in tonal region that I have pointed out. Such shifts in tonal center, or in 'tonality', or in 'key', are called 'modulations'; in the movement we have just heard, then, there are modulations from the key of D minor in [10] to B flat major in [11], then back to D minor in [12].* I should add what I have already said before—that it is the effect and your experience of the effect that are important, not the term 'modulation' or 'D minor'; and that I shall use these terms merely to identify effects that I point out for you to experience. And in Schubert's music the wonderful effects that he produces with his shifts in tonality are decidedly something for you to experience and for me to point out.

The modulations in [11] and [12] make their effect on ear and mind immediately; less immediately perceptible and effective are the long-range key-relations of the large sections of the movement. The exposition begins in B flat major, but modulates to F major; the development brings further modulations; but in the recapitulation the effect of the return to the opening theme is heightened by the return also to the original

* Music in the key of C major uses the mutually coherent sounds of this scale:

In C minor the series is:

The same major or minor series can start on D or B flat or any other sound.

key of B flat major, which this time is maintained to the end.

And now let us go on to the second movement of Schubert's Sonata. Its pace is, in contrast to that of the first movement, slow; its structure is what is called a 'three-part song form'—a cycle of which the middle part is not a further development of material of the first part, but instead deals exclusively with newly introduced material of its own. And the movement is deeply affecting—through its wonderful thematic ideas, and through its equally wonderful shifts in tonal position. Thus, the poignant opening theme:

which moves in the tonal region of C sharp minor, eventually builds up to a point of great intensity, which, as it is relaxed, leads to this passage:

in the tonal region of E major; and in implications there is a change at this point from poignancy to what can only approximately be described as suddenly achieved understanding and clarification. It is with these new connotations that the melody of [1] is repeated in the new tonal region of E major:

building up again to the point of great intensity, which, as it is relaxed, leads again to the melody of [2]:

shifted this time to the tonal region of the beginning of the movement, with a corresponding shift in implications from clarification back to poignancy which sinks into the blackest grief as the passage continues to the end of this first part.

With the beginning of the middle part there comes a shift in tonality from C sharp minor to A major, and in implications from grief to the all-comprehending resignation, strength and nobility conveyed by this theme:

which acquires urgency from the left-hand figuration. The theme is repeated with more rapid figuration in the right hand. Then a departure and return in the style of [5]; and a repetition of the departure in the style with the more rapid right-hand figuration, going on this time in a way that prepares you for something to come.

This turns out to be the return of [1], beginning the repetition of the first part of the movement. It is a repetition with changes. For one thing [1] is heard with a new figure in the bass, [a]:

which acquires the character of a powerful commentary. Also, when [1] has worked up to its point of great intensity, this is relaxed now into a new passage in the tonal region of C major which is a breath-taking surprise:

with new implications of understanding, resignation, sublimity. It is in C major that the melody of [1] begins to be repeated, soon shifting, however, to the [3] in E major and [4] in C sharp minor of the first part. But then the end is suddenly and wonderfully changed: from C sharp minor to [7] in C sharp major, and from poignant grief to understanding, noble resignation, sublimity.

In the third movement there is bubbling playfulness that justifies the term 'scherzo', which is Italian for 'joke'. The structure is the three-part cycle of 'scherzo with trio'—that is, scherzo-trio-scherzo (don't ask why, but just take 'trio' as the term for the middle part); and each part is itself cyclical, with an opening statement, a departure, a return, a repetition of the departure, and again the return.

The playfulness which manifests itself first in the opening melody over the bubbling accompaniment:

then begins to manifest itself in surprises; and with Schubert the surprises are mostly shifts in tonality that are breath-takingly miraculous in process and effect. Thus, the departure from [1]:

begins in E flat major, but begins to shift at the point marked with an asterisk, and reaches A flat major in the fifth measure. The repetition of [2] shifts in the same way to D flat major, which is the key of the passage that follows:

The repetition of [3]:

also begins in D flat major, but in the fourth measure it shifts miraculously to F sharp minor, and from there to its conclusion in A major, which is followed by other such shifts in the phrases that lead back to [1]. When [1] has run its course, [2] begins the repetition of the departure, which again leads back to [1].

The trio shifts from B flat major to B flat minor; and though the playfulness is clouded with melancholy it is still there, in the perverse accents of the bass, the surprise of the wonderful shift to D flat major at the point marked with an asterisk:

There is a departure, a return, again the departure, again the return. And then the scherzo once more, this time without the repetition of departure and return in its cycle.

After this playfulness a sharply struck octave, [a], dramatically compels our attention for the agitated and plaintive opening theme of the fourth and last movement:

as it does for each recurrence of the theme. A strange effect is produced by the fact that the tonality of the scherzo and of the present movement is B flat major, but the octave is a G introducing a theme which begins in C minor, and which barely reaches B flat major when the G breaks in with C minor again.

There is a brief departure, which begins to gather momentum and force, only to be interrupted by the octave introducing the return of [1]. Another departure is similarly interrupted; and [1] this time is carried to the beginning of a new train of thought in F major:

with the rapid right-hand figuration and syncopated bass producing an undercurrent of urgency and agitation under the lovely and wistful melody. This is elaborated extensively; then a stormy passage in F minor breaks in:

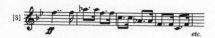

which continues with forceful developments, then quiet and exquisite ones—the last:

bringing the first premonition of the return of [1]. There are more such premonitions; and then the sharply struck octave breaks in, bringing [1], which begins a repetition of the entire sequence of ideas up to this point.

There are, then, in this movement, an exposition and a recapitulation without an intervening development; and the structure is called 'abridged first-movement form'. But there is some development in the recapitulation: the first departure from [1] is not brief this time, but an extensive development of the first measure of [1], with a tremendous climax that subsides into the sharply struck octave introducing the return of [1]. The rest follows as in the exposition without change except in key: the second departure from [1], and the second return; [2], now in B flat major; [3], now in B flat minor; the premonitions of the return of [1]; and the sharply struck octave bringing [1]. This time [1] is dramatically interrupted by a second sharply struck octave a half-tone lower than the first, introducing an altered statement of [1]; and this statement too is dramatically interrupted by a third sharply struck octave another half-tone lower, introducing another altered statement of [1], which this time continues further before it breaks off. A moment's silence; then a quick passage derived from [1] brings the movement and the entire work to an end.

Concerning the four-movement structure of the sonata Sullivan observes that "the general scheme of a first movement, usually representing a conflict of some kind, followed by a meditative or consoling slow movement, and that by a section easing the way to a vigorous final statement, to the conclusion won, is . . . admirably adapted to exhibit an important and recurrent psychological process." In this sonata of Schubert, it is interesting to note, the implications of final retrospective summation, clarification, resignation are in the first movement, and to a degree in the second, and there are implications of stress and conflict in the last.

I T is in his book about Beethoven that Sullivan makes his observation; and you will find that the observation applies to many of Beethoven's works. But it happens not to apply to the particular ones that we have considered. In the Sonata Opus 111 the psychological process is compressed into two movements: the conclusion you already know from our study of the second movement; and in the first you will now learn what preceded and led up to that final illumination. It is a movement which contrasts strikingly with the first movement of Schubert's sonata; for it is concise, compressed, brief in style and structure where the Schubert was expansive, and it is grim, violent, raging in implications where the Schubert was calm. The grimness and explosive violence are heard at once at the beginning of the slow introductory section; they flare up momentarily as this section becomes quieter with increasing suspense; and at the end the ominous trill in the bass explodes into this passage:

which hammers out first only a small part, [a], then a larger part, [b], and then all, [c], of the principal theme of the sonata-allegro movement that begins here. It is this theme that continues to be heard in an exposition in which violence subsides into momentary quiet only to flare up again; and a brief interlude of quiet:

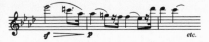

is broken into by further violence which culminates
in this upward rush to a sudden stop:

This concludes the exposition, which usually is repeated. The brief development of [1] works up with
increasing intensity to a vehement restatement of [1]
that begins the recapitulation. This time the concluding upward rush ends in a passage:

in which the violence at last spends itself. The brief
concluding passage that follows conveys exhaustion
after all this violence; then suddenly, in the sustained
C major chords and deeply solid bass figuration, there
is quiet, peace. And after the last C major chord you
hear next the opening C major chord of the great
theme of the second movement.

I commented only briefly on the concluding theme
and variations of the Sonata Opus 109; and I will
make only brief observations on the three movements
of the work as a whole. The extraordinary thing for

you to note in the first movement is the contrast between the extreme brevity and conciseness of its structure, and the spaciousness of its implications. The movement is quietly and wonderfully reflective; it is in the fast second movement that you hear some of the violence and fierceness you heard in the first movement of Opus 111; and these are resolved in the great concluding theme and variations of the last movement.

As for the Trio Opus 97 ('trio' here means a sonata played by three instruments), it is in four movements, but their scheme differs from the one Sullivan describes. The first movement is calmly and spaciously reflective, though with involvements that bring agitations, urgencies, tensions. Some of these occur, naturally, in the development, which is concerned chiefly with the beautiful opening theme; and they include one of the most affecting passages in the movement, derived from that theme:

and leading into a striking passage:

which begins quietly, but of which the trills [a] and the scale [b] acquire increasing momentum, sonority and intensity (the scale, for example, doubling its speed and changing from single to double notes on the piano), until they reach a climax that subsides into the return of the opening theme for the recapitulation.

The second movement is not the slow movement of the work, but its scherzo movement—unusual in the leisurely spaciousness of the development of its opening theme:

and in its somewhat ominous trio:

which is broken into repeatedly by a wildly boisterous episode.

After the scherzo comes the slow movement—the great theme and variations we studied earlier. And the concluding transitional chord that I mentioned brings us to a fourth movement which leaves profundity behind for a wistful sort of gaiety. Its structure is cyclical: a 'rondo', which keeps departing from the opening theme:

and coming around to it again.

THE great example of "a first movement, usually representing a conflict of some kind, followed by a meditative or consoling slow movement, and that by a section easing the way to a vigorous final statement, to the conclusion won," is Beethoven's *Eroica* Symphony (a 'symphony' is a sonata structure performed by an orchestra). Its first movement conveys—through its breathless urgency, its tremendous tensions and climaxes, its gigantic structure—the working out of a great dramatic conflict; and the exposition of thematic material is a statement of the elements of this conflict—very much like the first act of a play.

The urgency and tension are experienced at once

in the two opening chords like claps of thunder, which compel attention for the principal theme of the movement:

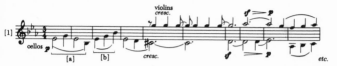

The theme begins quietly, but there is urgency in the rapid accompaniment, and tension starts with the cellos' C sharp, the violins' syncopations in the fifth measure, the *sf* accentuations a couple of measures later. A new theme:

creates more powerful shocks and tensions with the violent syncopated accents of the portion marked [a], which work up to a forceful statement of [1]. This breaks off for a theme:

which again is quiet, but with tensions in the plaintive fragments of the melody, and urgency in the agitated accompaniment, and with a final explosion that leads to another theme:

which likewise begins quietly, but works up to the violence of the short rhythmic figures in this passage:

It is carried to a climax which subsides for a quietly but poignantly reflective interlude:

Even in this, tension is built up in the crescendo to the *sf*. Its last grave echoing fragments lead to a passage:

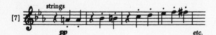

hushed, and made breathless through the rests in the first measures, before it gathers momentum and blazes up into this almost triumphant proclamation of strength:

It suddenly breaks into a rushing passage with powerful syncopated accents that culminate in tremendous rhythmic shocks and tensions:

These break off, but only for the phraseological tensions of this passage:

which work up to the vehemence of the exposition's conclusion:

The sudden quiet references to [1a] lead to a hush which creates increasing suspense, until it is broken by the beginning of the development.

In the development—with its references back to material already stated, its manipulation of this material and new material in progressions that work up to great climaxes—you get the involvements and crises of the drama, very much as in the later acts of a play. The first of these progressions begins with developments of [3], which subside into hushed developments of [1] that quickly blaze up into a combination:

which imparts to [1] the violence of the rhythmic figures of [5]. Then [12] breaks off suddenly for this passage:

only to break in again; and again it breaks off for [13], which now is carried to a climax—the climax of the first progression, and its end; after which the second progression begins. Like the first it begins with developments of [3], which now continue with increasing involvement and intensity to the beginning of this passage:

in which you experience again the powerful shocks and tensions created by the violent syncopated accents of [2a]. As the passage continues these shocks and tensions increase, until at the climax:

they reach a shattering maximum at the point (marked with asterisks) where they combine with the tensions of the dissonant juxtapositions of E and F. The tension is relaxed; and a third progression begins with a poignant theme that makes its first appearance in the movement at this point:

Vehement developments of [1] interrupt, but break off for [16] again, which leads now to this passage:

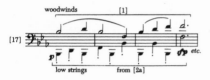

with tensions from the gigantic leaps in the bass that are worked up to another maximum point:

where there are the terrific tensions—after all the agitated movement—of the four sustained and accented chords, unsupported and maintaining themselves high up by their own inner force; and the equal tensions, down below, of the silence, then of the powerful three-note figure. These tensions are relaxed, in the repetition of the four measures, by the drop to *p*, then by the further decrescendo, the descent of the chords, the doubled speed of the three-note figure. There is a hush, suspense; a horn begins [1], only to be interrupted by an outburst from the entire orchestra; and this introduces the statement of [1] that begins the recapitulation.

It is a statement of [1] which, when it reaches the cellos' C sharp and the violins' syncopations in the fifth measure, resolves the tensions by a modulation, as breath-taking as one of Schubert's, into remote and serene tonal regions:

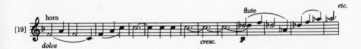

before the original stormy course of the material is resumed. The effect of a recapitulation can be a resolution of the crises of the development; in the present instance it appears to leave the elements of the conflict as they were. The sequence of material leads, as before, to the concluding vehemence of [11]; but the quiet references to [1] that follow now lead to a section of final summation (for which, you may as well learn at this point, the term is 'coda'), more extensive than any you have encountered, and bringing new involvements before it reaches final conclusions. And it is in this coda, like the epilogue of a play, that the conflict appears to be resolved at last.

It begins with [1a] in a new combination:

with new implications from the poignant figure [b] that work themselves out in the development of this figure. The development leads into [16], whose course is interrupted by [20b], which as it dies out creates suspense for the return of [17] in a new combination:

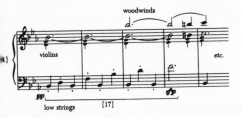

with the tensions of both bass and upper voice working up to a high point and then being relaxed. The last involvement has now been resolved; the rest is concluding affirmation, with [1] in a new combination:

building up with increasing intensity and sonority to last strong proclamations. These break off suddenly for a reference to [4], which quickly blazes up again into a last forceful passage with powerful rhythmic tensions that brings the movement to a close.

The second movement is a funeral march, as gigantic in structure and powerful in implications as the first movement. It begins with a poignant lament:

played first by the violins, with powerful comments by the string basses, and repeated by the oboe. Then the violins re-enter to carry the thought further:

with [a] beginning a transitional passage, increasingly hushed and dark, which is suddenly broken into violently by [1] in an altered form. All this too is repeated by the oboe. Then comes a passage:

beginning quietly but continuing with violent accentuations, that brings this first part of the movement to a conclusion.

Now comes the second part, in which the weight of grief and despair is lifted by a theme with consoling implications:

It leads to a strong outburst of the entire orchestra, and then is developed extensively and with increasing involvement before it ends once more in the outburst of the entire orchestra. This breaks off, leaving the strings to make a vehement descent into the depths of grief and despair again—to the point where [1] returns, apparently beginning the repetition of the first part, but bringing also the tremendous involvements and crises of the movement. That is, the conclusion of [1] brings an interruption by the two violently accented subjects of a fugal passage:

in which each successive statement of the subjects contributes to the gradual building up of texture, sonority, intensity to a tremendous climax. This breaks off with a great wrench; and you hear a fragmentary reference to [1], which the violins carry higher, reaching a point of motionless suspense. Suddenly cellos and basses break in violently, joined by more and more of the orchestra in a tremendous outburst, which gradually subsides into a poignantly accented figure that continues as an accompaniment to [1]:

in the repetition of the first part of the movement, which now continues without interruption.

Its conclusion is the beginning of the coda:

The violins' melody, which seems to reach a consoling conclusion after what has preceded, continues with powerful tension-creating inflections that die out into exhausted whispers. You hear [2a], hushed at first, then increasing in intensity and subsiding, its conclusion leading to a poignant outcry:

which is repeated, and in its repetition is elaborated

and intensified, subsiding into a last broken statement of [1] by the violins, which ends with a last cry from the entire orchestra and last powerful comments from the string basses.

After this comes the scherzo movement—with its exuberant playfulness, its joyousness, achieved on the same large scale as the conflict of the first movement, the grief and despair of the second. The playfulness, as in the scherzo of Schubert's sonata, manifests itself in surprise; and Beethoven's surprises are those of sonority and structure. Thus, for a long time the scherzo chatters along under wraps; and in this whisper its cyclical structure—of opening statement:

departure, carrying the same thought further, and return to [1]—is completed; whereupon it blazes up unexpectedly into an exuberant and extended statement of [1], and keeps going with new material, ending with a bang; after which the whispered departure again leads back to [1] and its extension.

Now the trio of the movement's larger scherzo-trio-scherzo cycle—the trio being a cycle of opening statement, with horns imitated playfully by oboes and strings:

departure, with the vigor of the full orchestra yielding to the suave fooling of woodwinds, then of strings:

and return to [2]; after which the departure again returns to [2].

And finally the repetition of the scherzo.

"His forms become more subtle as his animal spirits rise," remarks the great English critic Tovey of Haydn. It will repay you to look in Haydn's music for the confirmation of that statement, later on; right now you may observe how the exuberant energy and high spirits that were evident in the scherzo of Beethoven's symphony manifest themselves in a final movement which is one of the most extraordinary of all pieces of musical construction—extraordinary in the insignificance of the material it starts with, the profusion and variety of what it does with this material, the greatness it produces with the material in the end.

First you hear a loud introductory passage ending with many concluding flourishes, as though to prepare you for something momentous—and comparably loud—to come. And what comes—after this great build-up—is an absurdly insignificant passage plucked by the strings:

which is the first part of a theme that will undergo variation. And as if that were not absurdity enough it

is followed by the surprises—of silences broken now
by explosions, now by whispers—of the second part
of the theme:

There is humor again in the accompanying figure at
the beginning of the first variation:

and in the rest of the material that glides about the
theme. And all the chatter and darting about the
theme in the second variation is also amusing:

In the next variation [1] and [2] are combined with
the two parts of a charming melody:

and the second part is carried to the point where a fugal treatment of [1] begins:

with increasing involvement and intensity as it works up to a climax. This breaks off suddenly; but the excitement and urgency continue as the melody of [7] returns, is repeated in varied form, and continues with [8] in a double variation—first this light-footed gaiety:

then this bluster:

which continues, leading to [1] in a new combination with a vigorous dance-tune:

Instead of a variation of [2] you get this continuation of [12]:

which goes on with concluding flourishes that lead to a momentary pause. Once more the melody of [7] is heard; then involvement begins again as its first measures, combined with those of [1], are carried into different tonal regions in a premonitory hush, out of which there suddenly emerges the subject of the fugal passage, now inverted and made the subject of a new fugal passage:

in the course of which you hear a gay, rhythmically altered reference to [7], and at the climax the fugal subject proclaimed triumphantly in both uninverted and inverted forms. The climax increases in intensity, with concluding flourishes that prepare you for something momentous to come.

And this time, after a moment's silence, something

momentous does come: the melody of [7] in slow tempo, with implications of great solemnity and sublimity. Its two statements (first by the oboe, then by the violins) lead to this variation of the melody of [8]:

which is also repeated, leading to a majestic statement of [7] and [8]. This subsides into quietly retrospective reflections:

which lead to the beginning of new involvement—the rhythmic tensions of this new variation of [7]:

The involvement and urgency increase with the development of [17] and the faster pace, until a climax is reached, which breaks off for a dramatically hushed passage:

that creates increasing suspense—until suddenly the hush and suspense are broken by the loud introductory passage of the beginning of the movement, which this time continues with joyous references to [7] that are built up to a triumphant conclusion.

ANOTHER outstanding example of this four-movement scheme is Schubert's Symphony No. 9 in C major. In its first movement there is none of the breathless urgency and violent tensions that we heard in the *Eroica;* what it conveys is not conflict but involvement—involvement concerned with great issues. You know this from the solemn introduction, and from the wonderful pronouncement of the trombones late in the exposition:

which attains its full power in the tremendous climax of the development. (This climax breaks off for one of those passages with the instantaneously achieved intensities of loveliness and expressiveness which set one to hunting for words that will adequately characterize means and effect, and compel one in the end to express this in the word 'miracle'.)

Poignancy is conveyed by the oboe's theme in the first part of the second movement; the second part is consoling, and ends with one of the most wonderful of Schubertian miracles—the passage of transition:

back to the first part. And the course of the repeated first part is interrupted suddenly by a passage:

which—with the two-note figure [a] reiterated like a warning of doom—is carried with increasing urgency to shattering catastrophe and silence; after which a few mournfully retrospective measures lead to the consolation of the repeated second part, the poignancy again of the coda.

Music for the man who enjoys Hamlet

The scherzo follows, tremendous in structure and power—the power, for example, developed by the crescendo of this gigantic upward and downward swing:

that leads to the return of the opening theme.

And finally a movement which is one of the most extraordinary in all music in its sustained creative energy and in the magnificent power of what this energy produces. It is one of Schubert's rushing finales set off by an initial statement which keeps going with continuing impetus to the last chord—in the C major Symphony this initial statement:

whose sharp rhythm and whirl continue throughout the movement. And over the continuing whirl this statement:

with its reiterated opening notes, builds up to tremendous pronouncements in the exposition, the development, the recapitulation, and finally one of the greatest of codas—a crescendo of sharp rhythm, whirl and reiterated notes from initial dramatic hush to concluding radiance and exaltation.

IN striking contrast to this and the other exalted conclusions we have been concerned with is the despairing lament with which Tchaikovsky's *Pathétique* Symphony ends. That is one interesting fact about the work; but more important is the fact that what it communicates is powerful and affecting in the musical form in which it is communicated. That form is the product of dramatic imagination; of feeling for the entire complex of musical line, color, texture, mass; and of taste which uses these elements with economy, precision, discretion. And in it, one thing for you to note particularly is the color—as one element that heightens the effect of the others.

We have already encountered an example of this in the transition I pointed out in the second movement of Schubert's C major Symphony. The passage is wonderful even when played on the piano; but it is magical when the repeated G is that of a horn and the answering chords are those of strings. And in Tchaikovsky's *Pathétique* also there are superb musical ideas whose effect is heightened by their instrumental coloring. Listen, for example, to the melodic line of solo bassoon over accompanying string basses in the opening passage of the work, and note the shift of the melody to the violas for its climax. And when this passage is repeated, note at the end the sustained chord of low strings and bassoon, the entrance of the horn which releases this chord, the addition of the high woodwinds, then the horn an octave

lower, and the addition of low woodwinds and
violas. Listen, in the development, to the passage for
trumpet and trombones over the ominous rumble of
cellos and basses, with the rest of the brass joining
in as the passage begins to work up to a climax. Listen to the dramatically hushed passage after this
climax—to the sustained line of the trombone behind
the violins and violas, and its descending movement as
they begin to gather momentum:

with agitatedly repeated notes from the horns up
above and plucked notes from cellos and basses down
below. Listen, in the coda of the second movement,
to the descent first of the woodwinds, then of the
brass, against the ascent of the strings; and a little
later to the succession of solo woodwinds over strings.
Listen to the exquisite textures at the beginning of the
third movement. Listen, in the fourth movement, to
the bassoons and flutes which punctuate the first
lamenting phrases of the strings; as the strings continue note the continuing line of woodwind counterpoint; when the lamenting phrases return note the
punctuating bassoons, which continue to the beginning of the consoling second part. Note in this part
the tact with which the brass comments on the melody of the violins; and note that when the comment
is more powerful later on it is in proportion to the

power of the last statement of the melody. When the lamenting phrases return note that it is the horns that punctuate them; and that when, after the climax, the phrases are vehement the punctuating horns are raspingly muted. And listen to the passage for trombones and tuba that leads to the despairing conclusion.

Listen to all these details, and you will become aware of the many others. And you will realize that the imagination, the feeling for the medium, and the taste which produce the quiet passages I have mentioned also produce the tonal magnificences.

HAVING given ear to skill in use of the medium, let us go on to consider supreme mastery. No composer has produced phraseological contours as exquisite, textures as ravishing, forms as perfectly proportioned as those of Mozart. They may seem thin and pale, and what they communicate may seem insignificant, after the magnificent sonorities of Tchaikovsky, the immensities of Beethoven and Schubert. If they do, it means that you must listen long and attentively; then you will begin to perceive what powerful emotions are communicated in these forms of crystalline clarity and delicacy, and in time you will find the communication to be the more affecting for its subtlety, economy, concentration.

You will, that is, come to feel what expressive force is packed into the exquisitely contoured opening theme of the Symphony in G minor:

the force producing those first small eruptions [a], and the final large eruption [b], creating a tension which is released in the gradual descent of the remainder of the theme. Later—after the more obvious shocks of a forceful transitional passage—there are the expressive force, the tensions at the points marked by asterisks, in this theme:

and the ear is delighted not only by the contours of the melody but by the textures of strings and woodwinds in alternation. And similar contours, tensions, textures are to be heard a little later.

At the beginning of the development:

there are the marvelous sound and poignant effect of the shifts in tonality at the points marked with asterisks. These modulations are as wonderful as Schubert's; and I should say here that there is as frequent necessity for use of the word 'miracle' to describe instantaneously achieved intensities of loveliness and expressiveness in Mozart's music as in Schubert's. A forceful passage breaks in and leads to a succession of delicately wrought developments of [1] that are nothing less than miraculous in texture of sound and expressive effect:

Note sound and effect of woodwinds added to violins at the beginning; the sustained F of bassoon and clarinet down below in the second measure, its shift to G in the fifth measure; the addition of the lower strings in the eighth measure; their successive shifts to lower positions in the tenth measure and the twelfth. And after the powerful passage which breaks in there is the wonderful transition:

back to [1] for the recapitulation.

In the recapitulation note sound and effect of [2] in G minor (as against B flat major in the exposition):

And in the brief coda note the expressiveness and the tensions built up by overlapping statements of the variant of [1].

In the opening theme of the second movement:

there are the tensions built up by the successive entrances of [a], released in the exquisite contour of [b]; the tensions then of [c] and [d], with their characteristic Mozartian contours and poignancy. [a] and the initial two-note figure of [d] continue to be heard and to create such tensions throughout the movement.

In the third movement—in Mozart's day not a scherzo-trio-scherzo but a slower minuet-trio-minuet —the power of the opening statement of the minuet:

is increased in the departure:

by the clashing phrase [a]; and in the return:

by the overlapping statements of [1], which pile up tension-producing cross-rhythms, until suddenly the tumult breaks off for a conclusion that is another miracle of delicate texture with poignant effect. And in the trio there are more such textures.

In the finale, after the violence of the opening there is this passage to take note of:

with the characteristic contours, and their tensions and expressive effect; and particularly its conclusion:

with the sound and effect of the harmonic progressions at the points marked with asterisks. In the recapitulation this passage returns in G minor (as against B flat major in the exposition); and I give its four clauses in full in order to point out some of the things that make it one of the most wonderful pages in all music:

In *A* there are the exquisite contours and poignant effect of the melody; in *B* the rhythmic tensions of the reiterated D in the first two measures suddenly erupt into the violent distention of contour and agonized implications of the next two—all over marvelous harmonic progressions in the lower parts; in C there is a shift from textures of strings to those of woodwinds and horn, with even more marvelous harmonic progressions, including the breath-taking shift to A flat in the fifth and sixth measures; in D there are not only the melody of the woodwinds and the harmonic progressions of the low strings, but those poignant three G's of the violins in the third and fourth measures, which make the passage almost more than ear, mind and heart can endure.

O F the four passages of music with which you familiarized yourself early in the book, one remains—the piano's opening statement in the first movement of Beethoven's Piano Concerto No. 4. The formal structure of this movement is essentially that of the first movement of a sonata or a symphony, but with interesting features that result from its being—as its title surprisingly indicates—concerted music, and concerted music which employs the particular concerted procedure that has been called the 'concerto principle'. This procedure is the alternation, the opposition, the interplay of two groups of performers, one large and one small; and for an example of it in its early and simple form listen to the engaging first movement of Bach's *Brandenburg* Concerto No. 2.

In this piece the large group is the entire small orchestra of strings, flute, oboe and trumpet; the small group is a part of this large group—the flute, the oboe, the trumpet, and a single violin, which repeatedly

detach themselves from the orchestra. The entire
orchestra opens the movement with a buoyant and
brilliant passage, then breaks off for a contrasting
passage played by the solo violin; then the entire
orchestra breaks in with a part of its opening passage,
and again breaks off, this time for the solo violin and
oboe; again the orchestra breaks in with part of its
opening passage, and breaks off this time for the solo
oboe and flute; and so on throughout the movement
to a concluding restatement of the opening passage
by the entire orchestra. This opening passage which
keeps returning with the large group is called, logically again, the 'ritornello'.

After this listen to the first and last movements of
Bach's Concerto in D minor, chiefly because the work
is one of the greatest examples of Bach's large-scale
emotion working itself out into large-scale construction by means of astoundingly inexhaustible powers
of invention and manipulation—the continuing impetus and drive of the flood of ideas in the last movement being as breath-taking in its own way as that of
the finale of Schubert's C major Symphony. In addition there are these things to take note of: set against
the orchestra of strings is only one solo instrument,
whose solo passages in these two movements are more
extensive and richly elaborated than those we heard
in the *Brandenburg* Concerto. And the middle movement, which may need several hearings for you to
grasp, is something new for you in structure. A grave
opening statement by the orchestra is repeated as a
bass over which the solo instrument begins an eloquent dialogue with part of the orchestra; this bass
continues to be repeated, each time in a different key,

as a sort of ground-bass for the wide-ranging and ornate dialogue, giving it a coherent structural foundation; and at the end the solo instrument is silent while the orchestra repeats its opening statement, which is the more impressive for all that has intervened.

Turning now to the concerto of Mozart, you will find in it the concerto procedure integrated with sonata structure. Earlier you noted the dramatic implications of the sonata first-movement progression of exposition, development and recapitulation; now you will find that when the progression is the first movement of a Mozart piano concerto its dramatic character is heightened by the opposition of orchestra and solo piano. This opposition is intensified and made more dramatic by the fact that the orchestra is not just a group of strings, as it was in the Bach concerto, but strings and wind instruments which are themselves engaged in liveliest interplay; that this orchestra's opening ritornello is not the brief one of Bach but a necessarily extensive statement of some of the numerous themes of the sonata-form exposition; that being more extensive the orchestra's ritornello delays the entrance of the solo piano, and in so doing creates suspense in anticipation of this entrance; and that the solo piano, therefore, when it does at last make its entrance, must do what will justify the build-up and spotlighting and will make it stand out in sharp and effective contrast to the orchestra that has preceded it. And what raises the procedure to incandescence is Mozart's personal involvement in it—the fact that it is he who is matching himself, asserting himself against the orchestra.

Music for the man who enjoys Hamlet

Mozart, that is, wrote most of his piano concertos for the occasions when he presented himself to the public as the greatest musician of his time—the greatest pianist, exhibiting his brilliance and taste in performance in music especially written for the purpose by the greatest composer. He wrote a concerto, then, as an actor might write a play for himself to act in, or a dancer might compose a ballet for himself to dance in; and he produced a musical equivalent of these dramatic forms. The orchestra's extensive opening statement created the sort of suspense that is created by the minor characters or dancers who occupy the stage in anticipation of the entrance of the chief character or dancer; at its conclusion the orchestra bowed itself from the center of the stage to permit Mozart to make an arresting first entrance, to hold attention with exquisite melodies, brilliant passage-work, spirited dialogue with the orchestra, to impress, delight, provoke exclamation or applause, and to make a brilliant first exit; after which the orchestra's ritornello prepared for his next scene, and so on through the rest of the movement to the last ritornello, which paused on an inconclusive cadence to allow him to amaze the audience with his powers of improvisation in the 'cadenza', and which then resumed its course to bring the movement to a close. After this came the slow movement, which presented him as composer and performer of melody in sustained vocal style. And then a brilliantly gay finale, in which he could indulge his love of fun.

Writing for this purpose, writing with awareness of triumphs already achieved, with anticipation of triumph about to be won, he wrote with exuberance;

and Tovey's remark about Haydn applies also to Mozart, for whom, however, it must be amplified: as Mozart's spirits rise not only do his musical forms become fascinatingly subtle, but the substance that assumes these forms is an inexhaustible flow of such loveliness, such intense poignancy, such gaiety and wit, such dramatic power as only he has given us. And inexhaustible, also, is the variety of this substance; for in one concerto after another he wrote to impress his audience with his new and astounding ways of doing the same things. In this way he produced in the first movement of the Concerto K.595, for example, those bold modulations in the dialogue of piano and orchestra at the beginning of the development that must have taken his audience's breath away; or in the slow movement of K.467 that long, calm cantilena over agitated triplets and exciting plucked bass-notes, after which audiences today can be heard to take a deep breath. Indeed, opportunities for the fun he delighted in arose out of the fact that, writing for an audience which knew the formula he was using, he could play with his audience a little game of now doing what it expected and now doing the opposite.

You get, then, in the concertos not only some of Mozart's greatest utterances, but utterances as varied as the powerful first movements of the two concertos in minor keys, K.466 and 491, the lovely and wistful first movement of K.488, and that first movement of K.595, which is unique in its implications of late-in-life calm, with intimations of agony that preceded calm. And you get utterances not only as profound and pathetic, but as varied in their method, as the slow movements of K.453, 482, 488, and above all that slow movement of K.467.

CHOICE is therefore difficult; and if I choose for our consideration the Concerto K.453 it is because of the opening theme:

in which, it seems to me, are concentrated as in no other the qualities of feeling and style that are characteristic of Mozart—the chivalresque pride and grace communicated by the first sounds of the violins to [a]; the poignancy, at once intense and reserved, communicated by the exquisite curve upward and downward in the remainder of the violins' statement; the high spirits communicated by the punctuating flutters of the woodwinds. The movement, observes Tovey, is "in the most intellectual vein of high comedy"; but already in this first theme—so characteristic in its mingled poignancy and humor—you have an illustration of another observation by Tovey about Mozart—that the language of comedy is often the only dignified expression for the deepest feelings; and the movement will provide other illustrations of this.

The thought thus begun is continued by strings and woodwinds, until this forceful passage breaks in:

Its conclusion brings one of Mozart's comic touches: the pompous flourishes of the full orchestra; then the orchestra stopping while the bassoon chortles on by itself:

The other winds and the violins join the bassoon in what becomes a transition to this poignant theme:

It is repeated by the woodwinds with echoing figures from the violins; then suddenly the atmosphere darkens with suspense:

This is the first intimation of the approaching conclusion and new event; and the impression is strengthened by this statement:

which is repeated with marvelous descending counterpoint of woodwinds; and by further material, including finally this passage:

And then the piano enters.

It repeats [1]—with the woodwinds contributing their punctuating flutters as before; then—with wood-winds and strings joining in—it continues this line of thought, until the orchestra enters with [2], quietly this time, joined by the piano, which goes on with rapid passage-work (while strings and woodwinds are also active). This leads to the piano's statement of an entirely new theme which darts sharply this way and that in high spirits:

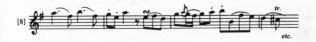

The repetition of [8], begun by the piano, is taken over by oboes and bassoons while the piano contrib-utes exquisite accompanying figures; these develop into passage-work which culminates in the piano's proclamation of the pompous flourishes of [3], con-tinued as before by the chortling bassoon; and again the other winds and strings join the bassoon in a transition to the piano's statement of [4]. It is re-peated by woodwinds with echoing figures from the piano, which then begins passage-work of increasing brilliance and momentum—against a background first of strings, then of winds—until the climactic moment when the piano makes its exit and the orchestra bursts in with [2] of the ritornello, followed by [7], which breaks off suddenly.

A moment's silence; then the violins usher in the first section of the development, in which woodwinds play phrases derived from [5], with the piano contributing ornamental figuration. The section ends with an outburst of pianistic brilliance; after which the violins introduce a new episode played by the piano:

with comments from the orchestra. As it continues it begins to create expectancy of some new event; and this proves to be the return of [1] played by the orchestra, which in this way begins the recapitulation.

The orchestra carries the ritornello—with a florid interjection from the piano—to the flourishes of [3]; and here Mozart contrives a surprise: instead of the chortling bassoon echoing these flourishes and leading to [4], it is the piano that takes them up and leads to [8]—after which the recapitulation follows exactly the course previously taken by the exposition from that point. Note, then, that in the exposition some of the thematic material stated in the ritornello was repeated by the solo piano, which also added some material that had not been stated in the ritornello; but that the recapitulation restates all this material more concisely—in the present instance omitting everything in the exposition between [3] of the ritornello and [8] of the solo portion.

Following the previous course of the exposition the recapitulation reaches the point where the piano makes its exit and the orchestra re-enters with the ritornello. And this time, after only a few measures, the ritornello pauses expectantly on an inconclusive cadence, and the piano re-enters for its cadenza. (In his own performances, as I have mentioned, Mozart improvised spontaneously on themes of the movement at this point; nowadays the pianist plays a cadenza that has been written out in advance. Mozart left written cadenzas for some of his concertos, including this one; and these should be used because they are in the same idiom and style as the rest of the work.) At its conclusion the ritornello resumes its course, and brings the movement to a close.

The slow movement, deeply affecting in implications, is extraordinary in form: several sequences of material, each of which takes its departure from the poignantly meditative statement, ending inconclusively in silence, that is heard at the beginning:

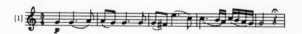

This first time it is played by the violins; and after the silence the first sequence begins with this melody:

in which there occurs the wonderful series of overlapping statements by the woodwinds, [a]. The thought is carried to the point where this vigorous passage:

breaks in, leading to a closing statement:

which is marvelous in its texture of strings joined by woodwinds, and moving in its pathetic implications.

Then the piano enters with the next statement of [1], ending inconclusively again in silence; and the second sequence of material begins with the piano's statement of this impassioned melody:

It leads into the woodwinds' overlapping statements of [2a], in which the piano joins, continuing the thought in a somewhat ornate style that elaborates and intensifies it. This leads to [4] from the woodwinds, in which again the piano joins; and the dialogue of piano and woodwinds builds up to the point where

Again [1] is heard, this time from the flute. And

after the silence the next sequence of material begins
with this poignant statement from the piano:

The piano's utterance becomes highly elaborated and
intensified through its ornate style; and at its conclusion the orchestra builds up to the point where

Again [1] is heard, this time from the piano, which
begins the next sequence of material with this imposing statement:

It leads to the woodwinds' overlapping statements of
[2a], in which the piano joins, carrying the thought
to the point where the orchestra breaks in with [3],
in which again the piano joins, carrying it to a conclusion. Then the orchestra briefly works up to a
pause on an inconclusive cadence, and the piano re-
enters for a cadenza. When it ends

[1] is heard again for the last time, from the woodwinds. But this time there is no silence: instead the
piano completes the thought with a statement that
has deeply affecting implications of summation; then
it joins strings and woodwinds in [4], which brings
the movement to a pathetic close.

And now follows the genial gaiety of this theme of
the finale:

and of several high-spirited variations; until suddenly all is dark and mysterious and ominous in this
variation:

with its tension-creating syncopations—first of strings
and woodwinds, then of piano, in the double variation
of each part. But the darkness and mystery are swept
away by the joyously brilliant variation which follows; its conclusion is continued by the piano in a
way that creates expectancy; and there is a pause.

Then begins a coda in the uproarious style of one
of Mozart's operatic finales. Over everything is an
atmosphere of exaggeration and extravagance, and
through these of mockery and absurdity. A bustling
theme of the strings, with over-excited comments
from horns and woodwinds:

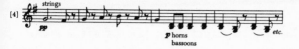

and with concluding flourishes, is repeated by the
piano with the same comments of horns and woodwinds. Brilliant flourishes reach a climax, from which
there is a sudden dizzying drop into hushed mock-
mystery and mock-dread:

followed by a crescendo to a climax that subsides
into a breathless reference to [1] by the piano, then
by the woodwinds. Again a climax and the dizzying
drop into the mock-mystery and dread of [5], and
the crescendo and climax which brought the reference to [1], but which this time bring instead another
crescendo and brilliant concluding flourishes. Then
at last, when you think the movement is over, you
get the piano's reference to [1], with a startlingly
unexpected and hilarious addition by the woodwinds
and horns; and it is with this comic stroke that the
movement ends.

TO come at last to Beethoven's Concerto No. 4: from its opening statement by the piano the work is Beethoven's adaptation for his own dramatic purposes of the dramatic form used so brilliantly by Mozart. For the first entrance of the solo instrument, as we have seen, was an important moment in the concerto progression, which Mozart therefore led up to with much care, and contrived with fresh ingenuity; and sometimes he contrived a surprise for his audience by entering slowly where it expected him to enter fast (Violin Concerto K.219), or by entering where it did not expect him to enter at all—in the very first statement of the orchestra's ritornello (Piano Concerto K.271). It was a surprise of this kind that Beethoven gave the audience assembled to hear him in the first performance of his Concerto No. 4—an audience which settled back expecting to hear the orchestra begin its ritornello, and which must have been startled by the unexpected and dramatically arresting opening statement of the piano. And on top of this shock came the shock of the change from the G major of the piano to the B major of the whispered answer of the strings.

From this point the progression is normal: the rest of the ritornello, and the entrance of the piano to complete the exposition; then the ritornello again, leading to the next entrance of the piano for the development, which builds up to the return of the piano's opening statement, amplified this time in rich chords and figuration that give it great force and impressiveness; then the rest of the recapitulation, and the ritornello again, which pauses after a few measures for the piano's cadenza; and then a conclusion played by piano and orchestra.

In the slow movement that follows, dramatically

imposing statements of the strings are answered by
the quietly reflective piano:

and the piano eventually takes over the stage for an
extended meditation in improvisatory style. Then a
hush, in which ghostly echoes of the strings' imposing statements lead to a quiet conclusion by orchestra
and piano. The movement is brief, but extraordinarily
spacious in its implications; and it is one of Beethoven's most remarkable and impressive utterances.

After this comes a lively concluding movement,
which requires no comment.

THE four movement sonata structure may
also be written for the two violins, viola
and cello of the 'string quartet' (like 'trio' the term
'quartet' refers to the group of instruments or performers, and also to the piece of music written for
the group).

We have noted in Mozart's music passages in which
the lines of sounds—of strings, of wind instruments,
of strings and winds—were combined in beautiful
aural textures. In a quartet of Mozart note the textures woven by the four strands of string tone—in
addition to which note the same implications of
pathos, of high-spirited gaiety, of dramatic power, as
are conveyed by his symphonies and concertos.

Thus, observe the exquisite texture created by the
progression of the four instruments in the opening

passage of the second movement of the Quartet K.458:

at the same time as you note the poignant implications of the first violin's melody, which are enriched by the other lines of sound. And the meditative third movement offers things as affecting as this melody:

and a little later this one, again with its implications enriched by the progressions of the lower voices:

The first and last movements, on the other hand, are delightfully high-spirited; and it is the gay opening passage of the first movement, suggesting a horn-call, that has given the work the title *Hunt* Quartet. This passage, having reached a first conclusion, starts again below a trill of the first violin, which then continues discursively with rapid scales that lead into a passage:

of which the first six measures lull you into complete unpreparedness for what happens in the succeeding measures: the apparent conclusion [a], with its little flutter played by the first violin, then echoed an octave lower each time by the second violin, the viola, the cello, all very dutifully, solemnly, and in the end comically; after which the four instruments scurry back upward after one another with the little flutter, even more comically. And that flutter continues to enliven the rest of the exposition—for example, this passage in which its effect is heightened by the sharp accentuations:

In the development too another mischievous and not unrelated figure:

works itself into involvements which suddenly give way to the triumphant "I fooled you" proclamation of [4a] again. (When it quiets down, a few transitional measures bring the return of the opening passage for the recapitulation.)

On the other hand the most intense melancholy and despair are to be heard in the Quintet in G minor (K.516). The fifth instrument is an additional viola, which for one thing enriches the texture, producing for example the intricacy and intensity of this passage at the beginning of the coda of the first movement:

And the additional viola also darkens the instrumental color of a work that contains the most anguished of Mozart's utterances—the slow third movement, and the slow introduction to the fourth movement. Beginning with this melody:

each step in the third movement brings something which pierces the heart anew—like this:

and this:

which continues with this:

103

and so on (in all these keep one ear on the lower parts). But the long melody of the introduction to the fourth movement communicates such agony, with such nobility and resignation in the telling, as would cause one to listen with averted eyes if it were something spoken by a living person. And even the minuet movement not only is extraordinarily poignant, but has an agonized intensity in its poignancy:

But more extraordinary is the minuet movement of the great companion Quintet K.515. There is, first, the sombre strangeness of the opening statement:

and what is developed from it. In the trio the flowing violin melody leads to a passage which conveys the strangeness in startling harmonic progressions and instrumental colorings:

And in the middle part of the trio come these violent
intensities:

The first movement of the work also is extraordinary
in its powerful style and implications—for example in
this opening theme:

and in the passage which concludes the exposition:

BEETHOVEN offers a more robust use of
the quartet medium to express what is expressed in the works of his in other media that we
have considered. Thus, the Quartet Opus 59 No. 3,
written during the same period as the *Eroica* Symphony, communicates in its four movements an emotional progression similar to that of the *Eroica*. In

the first movement, conflict—though without the *Eroica's* shattering intensities and climaxes—is embodied in a magnificent piece of musical construction, in which I will point out only the first *Allegro* theme that is heard after the mysterious slow introduction:

I do this to draw your attention to the two-note motive [a], which not only keeps recurring in new contexts in the exposition, but provides most of the involvements of the development, including this passage:

which is built up to a climax that breaks off for a trill by the first violin—this, in turn, leading into the violin's florid elaboration of [1], which begins the recapitulation.

The slow movement which follows is like nothing else in Beethoven in its strangeness, its "remote and frozen anguish"—the strangeness conveyed by this passage:

and what is derived from it; the anguish that begins to be conveyed by this theme with its violent intensities:

This quieter theme follows:

which ends in this one:

It is [2] that produces the involvements of the development, which quiet down eventually for [3] and [4]; and [3] the second time leads to a passage:

which dies out into a remote, breathless stillness over an ominous rumble of the cello. Then four equally ominous plucked notes from the cello; and [1] returns to begin the recapitulation.

An exquisite minuet leads through a transitional coda straight into the subject:

of the fugal opening section of the exposition of a triumphant concluding movement which is made breath-taking by the relentless drive of its energy.

On the other hand the Quartet Opus 132—one of the group of five quartets that were the last works Beethoven wrote—communicates the inner illumination and exaltation that we experienced in the concluding movement of the Sonata Opus 111. I have chosen Opus 132 for our consideration here because of its slow movement—because, that is, it offers in this movement an example of the variation process operating in the quartet medium, and achieving its end through elaboration and enrichment of texture; because the process is employed in a variation form of a type which we encounter for the first time; and chiefly because through the process and form you will apprehend one of the great contents of this period.

Opus 132 also offers the most intense communication of the pain which the last quartets convey with their exaltation—the pain which is communicated in the wonderful Cavatina in the fifth movement of Opus 130, and which tinges the gaiety of the extraordinary third movement. With Opus 132 there are relevant external circumstances which we may take note of: if it communicates pain so intensely, that is because Beethoven when he wrote it felt intensely the emotions of a man who had passed through a severe illness; and the great slow movement bears the superscription *Heiliger Dankgesang eines Genesenen an die Gottheit,* or *Solemn Song of Thanksgiving of a Convalescent to the Deity.*

The pain I have been talking about is communicated in the hushed, mysterious introductory measures of the first movement; and then more intensely in this opening theme of the *Allegro:*

It is communicated again in the first part of the second movement:

But then comes the middle part:

in which the first violin, playing at a great height and as though at a great distance, displaces the awareness of the pain of this earth with a vision of a celestial joy. It is, however, a vision which ends with the return of the first part.

And now the slow movement. Its variation form is one which Beethoven used in the slow movement of the Fifth Symphony, and in this last period also in the slow movement of the Ninth Symphony: a long opening statement, which is varied each time that it returns after a long alternating statement. Recollection of pain, mingled with the other emotions of a convalescent, is communicated in the first part, which begins with this sentence:

[1]

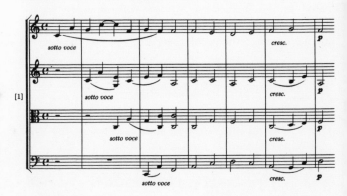

Note the first clause of quarter-notes creating a rhythmically active and intricate texture, and the second clause of half-notes creating a simple and solid texture and the effect of calm. The thought continues in further sentences with such first and second clauses. And at its conclusion the alternating part—which bears the superscription *Neue Kraft fühlend,* or *Feeling new strength,* and is in fact more vigorous and joyous—breaks in:

Its conclusion in turn brings the first restatement of [1], now varied:

Note the rhythmic elaboration [a], and the intricacy that it produces in the texture; and note also the continuation of this elaborated texture of the first clause below the sustained half-notes of the second clause. The alternating section again breaks in, itself varied, elaborated, intensified; and then comes the second restatement of [1], varied now in this manner:

Note the increased rhythmic elaboration, activation, intensification of the first clause; note the further elaboration [a] when this clause is combined with the sustained half-notes of the second clause, in [b]. It is with [b] that the thought continues, increasing in intensity, then subsiding to a momentary pause. Then the same train of thought begins again—the rhythmically elaborated figuration and the sustained half-notes increasing in intensity and carrying the illumination and exaltation to a climax of sheer ecstasy, where the figuration stops and only the solid texture of sustained half-notes is heard. The climax subsides—and as it does so the rhythmically elaborated figuration begins again; but the ecstasy remains to the last.

What Sullivan rightly calls a "forlorn and lonely little march" leads to a transition—full of dark terror and premonition—to the last movement, where again pain is communicated by the chief theme:

And it is not until almost the end that the emotional atmosphere changes: the pace accelerates to *Presto;* there is a last forceful statement by the cello of [1] in its original key of A minor, which suddenly subsides into this new theme in A major:

and from this point it is as though heavy black clouds had lifted and the sun were shining again after a long absence.

SCHUBERT'S great contributions to quartet music culminate in the Quintet Opus 163. I say 'culminate' because it is his last work in this medium, and because it is one which proceeds from the same fullness of matured emotional and musical powers, and achieves the same towering stature, as the other works of his last year of life that you have already learned to know—the Piano Sonata in B flat and the Symphony No. 9. It has moments of greater dramatic intensity than they; and its powerful sonorities are enriched and its color darkened by the second cello.

The dramatic intensity I have mentioned is heard in the first movement, after this quietly reflective opening:

Of the remaining material I will cite the closing theme of the exposition:

because it provides most of the involvements of the development, first quietly, then in a violent passage which quiets down for this beautiful and affecting development:

The sequence is repeated; and finally there is this powerful passage:

which subsides into an exquisite transition—with [4a] continuing to be heard—that leads to the return of [1]—with [4a] still continuing to be heard—and the recapitulation.

We come now to the slow movement, which is one of the most heart-breaking utterances in all music. Here is the beginning of its long first part:

Note the inner line of sustained melody played by second violin, viola and first cello, the poignant comments of the first violin, the plucked comments of the second cello. And here, after the agitated middle part, is the beginning of the restatement of the first part:

Note now the florid elaboration and intensification of
the comments of the first violin and the second cello.

The heart-breaking pathos does not end with this
movement. Completely unexpected in the buoyant
scherzo movement is the slow, sombre, strange, and
deeply affecting trio that begins as follows:

And sadness also clouds the gaiety of the lilting finale, as in this poignantly reflective passage:

A ND now a word about Haydn. "The essential character of Haydn's form is dramatic surprise at the moment," says Tovey; and "nothing in Haydn is difficult to follow, but almost everything is unexpected." Everything means melodic phraseology, harmonic progression, tonality, length of phrase, rhythm, accentuation, sonority, instrumental color. And what is unexpected always turns out to be not only logically right after what has preceded, but marvelously expressive and effective.

Let us follow the course of the slow introduction to the first movement of the Symphony No. 104 from one dramatic surprise to the next (see reproduction of score on pages 117 and 118). You hear first the entire orchestra in a forceful opening call and its answer, in the key of D. Then in the third measure comes the dramatic surprise, after this brilliance, of the dark D minor whisper of the lower strings, answered by the poignant figure [a] of the first violins; and you will note the powerful expressive implications of the statement as well as its startling unexpectedness. It is repeated in the fourth measure; then in the fifth it is repeated a second time—and this time with the next

Introduction to the first movement of Haydn's Symphony No. 104

surprise: the C natural at [b], which carries the passage expansively out of darkness into the light of F major, again with wonderfully expressive effect. It is in F major now, in the seventh measure, that you hear again the forceful opening call and its answer; and in the ninth measure comes the new dramatic surprise of the whispered E flat of the second violins at

[c], the 'diminished' chord of which it is part, the more poignant answering figure [a] of the first violins. The statement begins to build up in intensity, with [a] acquiring increasing urgency in the eleventh measure, and with the dramatic surprise in the twelfth of the sudden quiet in the upper voices while the cellos continue powerfully with [a] down below, contributing to the harmonic complexity that is resolved in the thirteenth measure. Again, in the fourteenth measure, the forceful opening call, this time back in the key of D; and now in the fifteenth come the most startling dramatic surprises of all: the hushed answer to the call, the G at [d] instead of A, the remote chord [e] which increases the atmosphere of mystery. In the sixteenth measure mystery gives way to expectancy, with the oboe contributing last poignant references to the answering figure [a]; there is a moment's silence; and then the first-movement *Allegro* begins.

The method is the same in fast tempo. Here is the lovely opening theme of the *Allegro:*

And here is what Haydn produces from its third and fourth measures at the beginning of the development:

Note that every phrase brings its surprise, every repetition its unexpected and expressive alteration. Note, when the first two measures are repeated, the change in harmony (marked by asterisk); note the next repetition, with its extension of phrase-length and new harmonic progressions; note the entrance of cellos and basses, introducing their dark color and making a striking harmony with the violins; note the entrance immediately afterward of flute and oboe, with their sharply contrasting woodwind color and the striking harmony they make with the strings; and so on in the remainder of the passage.

Haydn's method, then, is a constant playing with his hearers' minds; and as you listen to the first movement of the Quartet Opus 54 No. 1 or Opus 74 No. 2 you will become aware not only of the great emotional and technical powers but of the sheer high spirits that produce the breath-taking profusion of astounding and expressive details. Haydn is delighting in the powers which enable him to amuse himself by writing today what will startle his hearers and move or delight them next week. On the one hand, then, he carries the beautiful second movement of the Symphony No. 104 through most of the restatement of its first part, and suddenly takes it off on the series of wonderful wide-ranging digressions that begin with

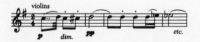

And on the other hand he ends the minuet of the third movement with this musical equivalent of a bit of slapstick comedy:

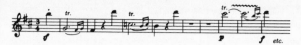

that is, with the silence where you expect the trill, and then *piano* where you expect *forte*.

WE turn now to music associated with words. In the beginning I pointed out that we listened to Beethoven not merely for his insights but for these insights made explicit in a particular construction in sound—for the same inner illumination and exaltation made explicit in a number of different constructions in sound. And now I might point out that we listen to Schubert's song *Litanei* or *Nacht und Träume,* or *Des Fischers Liebesglück* not merely for the meaning of the words but for the form in sound in which that meaning is made explicit—for the implications conveyed by the music that are not conveyed by the words.

The association of music with words in a song is something you probably accept as making sense; indeed you may have accepted it when you thought music without words in a sonata made no sense. On the other hand music associated with words in an opera may strike you as absurd; but if a song doesn't strike you that way, neither should an opera.

Consider Schubert's song *Gretchen am Spinnrade.* You hear first a piano figuration which suggests the whirring of Gretchen's spinning-wheel, and which continues below her voice as she tells of her peace that is gone, her heart that is heavy, her mind that is distraught. You hear her growing excitement as she recalls her departed lover's noble figure, his smile, the power of his eye, the enchantment of his speech, the pressure of his hand, his kiss—at which climactic point the music breaks off dramatically. Gradually the piano resumes the movement of the spinning-wheel; again Gretchen tells of her peace that is gone; and again the music rises to a climax as she longs to hold her lover, to die of his kisses. The music becomes quiet as once more she tells of her peace that is gone; then she is silent, and the piano's whirring stops.

The Gretchen of this song is the Gretchen of Goethe's *Faust*; and the music you have heard deals effectively, and acceptably to you, with one situation in the play. Schubert might have written music for the other situations that would have been acceptable to you; why should it have been less acceptable if it had been sung on a stage? You may say that what happens on a stage is too close to reality for you to be able to accept anything as unreal as someone singing his thoughts to himself or to someone else. But if you can accept the conventions involved in Hamlet's speaking his thoughts about suicide in blank verse, you should be able to accept the additional convention involved in Boris Godunov's singing his tormenting thoughts about his crime. Try listening to his monologue in Mussorgsky's opera *Boris Godunov*, and see whether it does not justify itself to you— whether, in fact, what Boris thinks is not more dramatically effective and moving as he sings it and the orchestra underlines it, than it would be if he merely spoke it.

You hear phrases of the orchestra which seem to tear at Boris's soul as, overcome by Shuisky's description of the murdered tsarevitch, he sinks into a chair. He was suffocating, he exclaims. Oh! how his conscience punishes him! The orchestra begins music that is sinister, eerie, as he recalls the torments which a single misdeed can bring (Chaliapin, here, does not sing the written notes, but declaims them freely)—the suffocation, the visions of the murdered child. Suddenly, in an ominous stillness he thinks he sees the child: "There! What is that? Over there?" And as the orchestra begins the most terrifying crescendo in opera he cries out to the child to be gone—that it is not he who is guilty of the murder, but the people that willed it. The shattering climax spends itself; the hallucination is over; and exhausted he asks God, who will not let him die, to have mercy on Tsar Boris.

If you can accept Boris's monologue, listen now to *O patria mia* in Verdi's *Aïda,* in which thought and emotion are expressed in formalized melody. In agitated declamatory phrases Aïda utters her fear that Rhadames is coming only to bid her farewell. If so, the dark Nile (note the surging flood of low string sound) will receive her body; and she will find peace. A plaintive melody of the solo oboe leads to her mournful exclamation: "O my country (*O patria mia*), no more will I see thee!" and to the lovely melody, exquisitely accompanied by a tremolo of flutes over plucked cellos and basses, in which she recalls the beauties (*O cieli azzuri*) she will see no more. Again the melody of the solo oboe and her mournful exclamation, which lead to a repetition of the lovely melody (*O fresche valli*), accompanied this time by agitated figures of the strings. The melody is carried to a climax, and a conclusion.

And now try listening to *Ah! fors' è lui* in Verdi's *La Traviata,* in which the formalized melody breaks out into florid passages that may strike you as too artificial and exhibitionistic to be taken seriously. But you have had occasion to note the emotional intensification produced by ornate elaboration of melodic line; and you will find that Violetta's florid style is related to her emotion. In the agitated declamatory phrases that you hear first she wonders (*È strano! è strano!*) at the new emotion she feels. Shall she accept it, or reject it? Then begins the melody in which she asks (*Ah! fors' è lui*) whether this is the man she dreamed of meeting some day—a melody which culminates in her declaration that this is love (*A, quell' amor*). And it is the intensity of her emotion that expresses itself in the florid passage at its conclusion. But in agitated declamatory phrases she tells herself that these thoughts are folly (*Follie! follie!*): she is alone, weak, friendless in this great city; what can she hope for? Only pleasure (*Gioire!*), to which she will abandon herself. And it is her feverish, desperate emotions that produce the florid outbursts here and in the melody (*Sempre libera*) in which she repeats at length her decision to pursue pleasure.

Perhaps by now you accept the sung monologue and dialogue; but the idea of five people singing their thoughts to the audience at the same time is one that you find ludicrous. The fact is, however, that in life a tense scene or animated discussion is likely to leave five people carrying on their five private trains of thought simultaneously; and the quintet in the third act of *Die Meistersinger* conveys a reality which the spoken drama is unable to convey.

Though I have directed your attention to orchestral details in the music of *Boris Godunov* and *Aïda* I have spoken mostly about the vocal parts. Let me therefore emphasize the fact that you must listen not only to the voice but to the orchestra—not only to Leporello singing the *Catalogue Aria* in Mozart's *Don Giovanni*, but to the subdued mischief of the detached sounds of violins, answered by cellos and basses, accompanying his *Madamina! il catalogo è questo*; the gleeful outburst of violins and woodwinds introducing his *In Italia sei cento e quaranta,* and the repressed chatter of winds accompanying the statement; the suave comment of violins after his emphatic *Ma in Ispagna son già mille e tre*; the descending scale of violins, like repressed laughter, introducing the repetition of *In Italia,* and the answering ascending scale of cellos and basses introducing *sei cento e quaranta*; and so on.

The orchestra not only comments on, and underlines, and creates the atmosphere for what is said and done on the stage; but while the curtain is down it prepares your mind and emotions for what you will see and hear when the curtain rises. Listen to the Preludes to the third acts of *La Traviata, Tristan und Isolde* and *Die Meistersinger*; and note how each prepares you, after what has happened, for what is to come. In *La Traviata* it will be the pathetic end of the courtesan whom you have seen so gay, so noble, so wronged; in *Tristan und Isolde* the desolate scene, the bodily illness of the wounded Tristan, his spiritual sickness at heart; in *Die Meistersinger* the saddening wisdom and greatness of soul of Hans Sachs.

YOU should now be in the right frame of mind to listen to one of the greatest wonders achieved by human powers, Mozart's opera *The Marriage of Figaro,* with proper appreciation of its forms in sound and what they express. For one thing Leporello's aria has taught you to keep an ear on the running fire of comment from Mozart's orchestra; and you would do well to go through *Figaro* once listening only to the orchestra: after giving your attention wholly to its innumerable exquisite and witty details you will continue to be aware of them when you listen to the voices. And I hope that Leporello's aria also has taught you the expressive intensity of what Mozart wrought with delicacy, economy and subtlety—something which ears accustomed to modern sonority and vehemence are in danger of missing. Then you will perceive Mozart's complete adequacy for any demand of the drama he is setting—for the sorrow of the neglected wife in the Countess's *Porgi amor* and *Dove sono*; the longing of Susanna's *Deh vieni, non tardar*; the amused tenderness of her *Venite, inginocchiatevi*; the confused adolescent emotions of Cherubino's *Non so più cosa son*; the ironic menace of Figaro's *Se vuol ballare*; the mock heroics of his *Non più andrai*; the pompousness and malice of Bartolo's *La vendetta*; the humor and wit of the opening duets of Susanna and Figaro, the *Crudel! perchè finora* duet of Susanna and the Count; the comedy of the *Cosa sento!* trio, the great finale of Act 2, the finale of Act 4; the sublimity of the end.

The Overture is as light and transparent as air, and so swift that it is hardly begun when it is already ended; but it may leave you shaken by an impact that would not be greater if the piece were louder. A little later Cherubino, in the course of his first aria, returns to the opening stanza, *Non so più cosa son,* which ends with the words *Ogni donna mi fa palpitar;*

and then comes a transition to *Parlo d'amor vegliando* in which all that happens is a change of harmony in the sustained chords of the few winds, with exquisite accompanying figures in the violins:

but the effect would not be more overwhelming if it were made with all the harmonic and orchestral luxuriance of Wagner or Strauss.

Much later, in the second-act finale, there is this astoundingly achieved expression of the emotions of the Count and the Countess as Susanna unexpectedly emerges from the cabinet:

And Mozart's resources are ample for him to carry off all the subsequent involvements of that finale with ease and brilliance. For example, the bland irony in Susanna's reply to the amazed Count and Countess, *Signore! cos' è quel stupore?*; and a moment later the spellbound wonder conveyed by the voices of the Count and Countess and the descending scale of violins and bassoon, while Susanna chuckles to herself as she looks on:

Then the long fast-moving passage, with the orchestra providing an atmosphere of high comedy, the Count imploring, the Countess and Susanna chattering their prim severity:

Le vo - stre fol - li - e non mer - tan pie - tà, *etc.*

Figaro's entrance provides a brief lower-comedy interlude; then high comedy is resumed with the menacingly stately melody of the Count's *Conoscete, signor Figaro, questo foglio chi vergò?*:

and the suavely impudent comment of the violins behind Figaro's *Nol conosco*:

The gardener Antonio's entrance brings, in his *Dal balcone che guarda in giardino*, a marvelous musical characterization of stolid stupidity in a state of excitement, which is burlesqued a moment later in Figaro's *Via piangione, sta zitto una volta*. And Figaro's *e stravolto m'ho un nervo del piè* introduces this figure:

with which Mozart builds up breathless suspense as the Count interrogates Figaro—to the point where Figaro's *è l'usanza di porvi il suggello* carries suspense to triumph:

And with his own resources Mozart can achieve this sublimity at the end of the opera:

THERE is, finally, 'program music', which conveys visual images, ideas, the incidents of a narrative. And again I might point out that we listen to Beethoven's *Pastoral* Symphony or Strauss's *Don Quixote* or Berlioz's *Queen Mab* or Debussy's *Nuages* not merely for its programmatic meaning, but for the particular piece of musical construction in which that meaning is made explicit—for the implications conveyed by the music that are not conveyed by the sights and sounds of the country, by Cervantes's book, by Shakespeare's poem, by clouds moving across the sky. Pieces of program music begin by being pieces of music—in most instances constructions in sound of the kinds you have come to know, which often can be listened to and enjoyed as such even without knowledge of the programmatic ideas and involvements that are embodied in the themes and their manipulation.

If we except a few literal imitations of bird-calls at the end of one movement and a musical representation of a storm in another, Beethoven's *Pastoral* Symphony is pastoral only in a generalized way—only insofar as it uses thematic material in an idiom which has pastoral associations for us; and aside from this it is to be taken as another Beethoven symphony. The first movement has the superscription *Awakening of cheerful feelings on one's arrival in the country*; but with the country indicated only by the pastoral idiom of its thematic material, the emotions are only those conveyed by the formal relations of a normal first-movement structure. The second movement is a *Scene by the brook*; but the brook is present only as the gentle flow and murmur of the strings below another first-movement structure which conveys the emotional implications of the movement. The *Merry gathering of country folk* of the third movement is indicated only by the country dances that are used in this scherzo. As for the fifth movement—*Shepherd's song: Joyful, thankful feelings after the storm*—the scene again is indicated by the pastoral idiom of the thematic material, and the emotions are those conveyed by the formal relations of the first-movement structure.

On the other hand Strauss's *Don Quixote* gives us incidents from Cervantes's book; but these too are conveyed in a theme-and-variations structure; and many of the marvelous strokes of humor and wit are achieved by the variation process applied to the themes which characterize Don Quixote, Sancho Panza and Dulcinea. They are achieved also by use of the orchestra—by such things as the grunting bass tuba to speak for Sancho Panza, the glissandos of the harp to convey the Don's giddiness at the thought of Dulcinea while he keeps knightly vigil. That is something new for you, which calls for a few remarks by me.

These remarks, however, will be concerned not with Strauss's use of the orchestra, which you will have little difficulty in appreciating, but with Berlioz's, which is more subtle and elusive. It is in fact an integral part of an entire musical idiom unlike anyone else's in its turns of melody, its progressions of harmony, its instrumental colorings—all the product of a highly individual mind and individual sense for the medium. Berlioz's is not only a fascinatingly original mind but a poetic one; and for its purpose of poetic suggestion it uses its musical medium with extraordinary finesse and subtlety. You can hear all this in the frequently played pieces from *The Damnation of Faust:* the *Dance of the Sylphs* (note, among other things, the sounds of the harp) and the *Minuet of the*

Will-o'-the-Wisps; but for an example of Berlioz's imagination and method operating at incandescence listen to the *Queen Mab* movement from *Romeo and Juliet*.

The piece is subtitled *The Fairy of Dreams*; it is also described as a scherzo; and like the first movement of Beethoven's *Pastoral* Symphony it elaborates into a formal structure a number of thematic ideas appropriate to its subject. There is this difference, however: Beethoven adapts to his own ways of thinking and writing the conventional pastoral idiom that lies ready to hand; whereas Berlioz invents the appropriate idioms and styles for his subject—the tiny supernatural creature who dashes from sleeper to sleeper in her chariot made of an empty hazel-nut. The atmosphere, the sights, the sounds of a fairy world are what the piece conveys; and here are examples of the tonal magic with which it does this.

The first is the opening:

Music for the man who enjoys Hamlet

the evocative chords of woodwinds alternating with muted violins; then the playful alternation of string staccatos and trills with woodwind, until the muted violins begin their upward rush [a], with interjections [b] and [c] from other strings and woodwinds. All these are mere preliminaries, which are repeated, until at last [1a] begins to function as the theme of an extended section, in which the woodwinds now contribute sharp glints of color, now interject a playful staccato chord amid the riotous rush and chatter of the muted strings, and now rush and chatter themselves.

Eventually this first section ends on a long trill of the first violins, which continues as the accompaniment of this melody of flute and English horn:

At [a] note the echoing violas and cellos, and the entrance of gleaming harmonics of the violins; at [b] the sounds of the harps, and the violas entering with a reference to [1a] and continuing to dart about below the calm melody.

[1a] returns with the first section; but soon a new section begins with this theme from a distant horn:

and with the irrepressible strings commenting with
references to [1a]. Note each subsequent entrance of
the horns, with the comments from strings and woodwinds; note the sudden hush, the breath-taking *pp*
entrance of the kettledrums leading to magically distant horns, the blazing up of the entire orchestra, the
horns again, another blazing-up of the entire orchestra, breaking off for a long *ff* tremolo of violas. This
tremolo drops to *pp* as chords of muted strings and
woodwinds are heard.

And now this section:

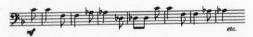

extraordinary in the ostinato theme of the clarinet,
the gleaming color of the accompanying harp; in the
gradual enrichment of the theme by the English horn,
of the accompaniment by the second harp and the
silvery antique cymbal; in the sudden breath-taking
splendor when the other woodwinds and the strings
enter.

[1a] and the first section return very briefly; there
is a retardation, a dying down to wonderful hushed
chords of muted strings, which lead to a passage rem-
iniscent of the preliminaries, with implications this
time of an approaching conclusion: the alternations
of evocative woodwind and string chords; then strings
punctuated by silvery antique cymbals; then staccatos
from woodwinds, strings, harps. And then last rushes
of [1a] bring the piece to a close.

THERE is tonal magic, differently contrived,
also in Debussy's *La Mer*, to suggest the
atmosphere, the sights, the sounds of the sea. It is a

work that you must not miss; but you would be wise
to defer it until you have listened to other music a
long time, and to Berlioz's *Queen Mab,* which departs
from Beethoven and Mozart and Schubert enough to
prepare your ears and mind for music which departs
from them even more. Though the substance of *Queen
Mab* is strikingly different from Beethoven's and
Schubert's, it has the same type of continuity of melody, development and structure as you have become
familiar with in their music. But in *La Mer* you may
be bewildered at first not only by a substance as individual in its own way as Berlioz's, but by the absence of the procedures of musical thought, and the
continuities resulting from these procedures, that you
have become accustomed to. You must now accustom
yourself to a substance consisting of mere fragments
of melody, of figuration, of color; and to a progression which pieces these fragments together into a
coherent, marvelously evocative, and magnificent form
in sound.

La Mer is a comparatively late work of Debussy in
which, as in *Ibéria,* you hear the method at its point
of highest development, producing the richest and
most complex structure, the most intricately integrated
structure. You might therefore begin with the early
Nuages, which is intended to suggest clouds moving
across the sky; for its opening page gives you the
simple beginnings of the method in the statement of
the thematic fragments and bits of color that create
the atmosphere of the scene (note the change to G
sharp in the violins at [a], the reduction of chord to
octave at [b]):

but the first woodwind theme is fairly extensive and continues by the kind of elaboration you are accustomed to, as does the later theme of the solo flute and harp; and the fragmentary recurrence of the opening material at the end gives you an approximation of cyclical structure.

After this listen to the substance and texture of the second movement of *La Mer*. You will have to become familiar with the detail by long and attentive listening; but it falls into several sections, which I suggest that you get to know one at a time; and here are the important themes with which the sections begin. The first, after the brief introduction, is

The next is

The next is

which introduces a long series of details of the "play of the waves" that this movement is concerned with. These culminate in a blazing-up of the entire orchestra; and then [2] returns, starting a crescendo to the climax of the movement, which subsides into concluding fragments of substance and color.

I THINK we have reached the point where you can go on by yourself; and I will merely add a word about performance.

When you look at a Cézanne still-life you see what Cézanne himself painted. When you listen to a reading of a Shakespeare sonnet or when you read it yourself you get Shakespeare's sequence of words, but in a precise form created by the inflection they get from the speaker or yourself. And so with music: you hear a Beethoven sonata only in the form in sound which it is given by some pianist; which means that the implications and effect of the sonata, like those of the poem, depend on how it is performed.

Beethoven, when he created the complete detailed form in sound in his mind, wrote down on paper a series of symbols which were to convey this imagined form to the performer, whose function it would be to produce the form in actual sound. It is true that the symbols cannot convey the form exactly as Beethoven imagined it; they convey only an approximation, to which the performer must give the final sharp definition and contours. But the fact that the symbols are not sufficient for the performer to produce the form in sound entirely as Beethoven imagined it does not free him of the obligation to produce it to the degree to which Beethoven's symbols do convey it. That is, it is not true that Beethoven merely provides sounds with which the performer is free to create any shape he likes: he has no more right to change the composer's scheme of sonority and pace than anyone would have to alter the shape of one of Cézanne's pears. He must produce what the printed score directs that he produce; and it is to this that he must add what the printed score cannot convey—the final contours which represent his own feeling for the medium and his own imaginative insight.

As for these, listen to Toscanini's performance of the Prelude to Act 3 of *La Traviata*, and note how the sound proceeds in time with slight accelerations and retardations of pace and with expansions and contractions of sonority. These produce the inflection, the phrasing, the contour of the melodic line, the shaping of the tonal mass. The continuum of sound moving in time is a plastic medium; and the changes in pace and sonority represent a plastic sense operating on this medium—a plastic sense which shows itself in the fact that each change is correctly proportioned to what precedes and follows, making the form coherent and continuous, with the timing and force of one sound implying the timing and force of the next.

The form created by Toscanini is not only plastically beautiful but right in emotional implications; the performance represents not only his plastic sense but his imaginative insight. Listen to that opening statement of the piano in Beethoven's Concerto No. 4, which Schnabel's performance makes deeply and spaciously meditative; and listen to it played by Gieseking—to the brisk pace, the brittle staccatos that make the statement the opposite of deeply and spaciously meditative. Note how Schnabel's inflection of the statement builds up and releases powerful tensions in the movement toward and away from salient points in the contour of the phrase; note throughout the work these tensions and momentums of the powerfully detailed phrasing that probes deeply into the music; and note, on the other hand, Gieseking's swift, smooth, plastically rounded and finished phrasing which remains on the surface of the music. Gieseking's performance reveals an inadequacy of imaginative insight in this work—though there is other music in which his insight is superbly adequate.

It is not true, then, that two different performances by two celebrated performers must be accepted as equally valid. If, for example, there are breathless urgencies and tensions and intensities in the first movement of Beethoven's *Eroica* Symphony, then Toscanini's recorded performance with its breathless urgencies and tensions and intensities, and Walter's recorded performance with its slackness and nervelessness, are not equally valid.

The way for you to learn to appreciate good performance is to listen to it. Listen long enough to the performances of Toscanini, Casals, Schnabel, Cantelli, Flagstad, Steber, Bjoerling, and you will acquire an understanding of, and distaste for, the vehement plastic distortions of Koussevitzky, the sensationalism of Stokowski. You will learn, that is, not to be excited by mere technical brilliance to the point of mistaking it for good performance. A pianist or violinist must be able to play his instrument, a conductor to get his orchestra to play with precision and beauty of sound; but such technical competence, however impressive, only provides the means for him to do his real job as a musician. You will marvel at the gorgeous sounds that Stokowski produces with an orchestra; but you will know that if these sounds give a Bach Chorale-Prelude or Mussorgsky's *Boris Godunov* the feverish excitement of Wagner's *Tristan und Isolde,* the performance is a bad performance.

AS for what to read about music—the important thing in criticism is not the mere opinion that this piece of music is good and that one is bad, or that this is a good performance and that is a bad one, but the reasons for the opinion; for in these reasons the critic applies to what he has heard (when he has heard what he is writing about) the illuminating insights (when he has such insights) that make him valuable to his readers. The only writing worth your attention, then, is that of the person who has listened to music with the capacity to hear what he has listened to, and with insights that enable him to point out in the music things which you would not perceive for yourself.

You will find such writing in Sullivan's *Beethoven,* Turner's books on Mozart, Beethoven and Berlioz, Dent's *Mozart's Operas,* Wotton's *Hector Berlioz,* Toye's books on Verdi and Rossini. You will find it in Tovey's writings on Haydn, Mozart, Beethoven and Schubert in *Essays in Musical Analysis* and *The Main Stream of Music* (though these require considerable technical knowledge to be understood completely). You will find it in some (but not all) of the musical journalism of Virgil Thomson collected in *The Musical Scene, The Art of Judging Music* and *Music Right and Left.* You will find it in Berlioz's essay on Rossini's *William Tell* (included in Strunk's *Source Readings in Music History*) and in the occasional observations on music in the *Memoirs* and

Music for the man who enjoys Hamlet

Evenings with the Orchestra by this great composer who was one of the greatest music critics—by virtue not only of his critical perception and literary brilliance but of his integrity in relation to his material, and the personal intensity, passion and greatness of spirit that come through so movingly in the operation.

And you will find it in the four volumes (published in England) of Bernard Shaw's *London Music in 1888-1889, as Heard by Corno di Bassetto* and *Music in London 1890-1894* (which you should read in preference to the paperback volume with a badly made selection from the four). It may surprise you to learn that Shaw did music-reviewing of this kind; but the fact is that he produced in his reviews some of the finest writing on music that I know of; and you would do better to read his reviews of those events of seventy years ago than to read the review of yesterday's concert in your newspaper. The performance of Boito's *Mefistofele* which Shaw wrote about on May 29, 1889, is of no interest to you today; but it provided the occasion for him to observe that Gounod's *Faust* was "a true musical creation, whereas Boito has only adapted the existing resources of orchestration and harmony very ably to his libretto. In short, Gounod has set music to Faust, and Boito has set Faust to music"; and that "the house likes Boito's prologue, in spite of the empty stage and the two ragged holes in a cloth which realize Mr. Harris's modest conception of hell and heaven." This is not the best but merely the shortest illustration of the fact that the daily events of the musical season elicited from Shaw a flow of comment on music, on musical performance, on the entire musical scene, that is still among the most discerning, the most instructive, the most enjoyable you can read in any language.

RECORDED PERFORMANCES
OF THE WORKS DISCUSSED

BACH

Concerto in D minor. Sylvia Marlowe and Concert Arts Chamber Orchestra: Capitol P-8375.

Brandenburg **Concerto No. 2.** Busch Chamber Players: Angel COLC-13. Goldberg and Netherlands Chamber Orchestra: Epic LC-3604 (mono) and BC-1043 (stereo).

Passacaglia. Walcha: Decca ARC-3021.

BEETHOVEN

Sonata Op. 111. Watch for the reissue of the Schnabel performance formerly on RCA Victor LCT-1109. Glenn Gould: Columbia ML-5130.

Sonata Op. 109. Watch for the reissue of the Schnabel performance formerly on Victor LCT-1110. Myra Hess: Angel 35705.

Variations on a Waltz of Diabelli. Watch for the reissue of the Schnabel performance. Leonard Shure: Epic LC-3382.

Trio Op. 97. Cortot, Thibaud and Casals: Angel COLH-29. Istomin, Schneider and Casals: Columbia ML-4574.

Concerto No. 4. Watch for the reissue on Angel COLH-4 of the post-war Schnabel performance formerly on Victor LVT-1010, and the possible reissue of the pre-war Schnabel performance formerly on Victor LCT-6700. Leon Fleisher and Cleveland Orchestra under Szell: Epic LC-3574 (mono) and BC-1025 (stereo).

Music for the man who enjoys Hamlet

Symphony No. 3 (*Eroica*). Toscanini and NBC Symphony: Victor LM-2387, which is to be preferred to LM-1042 and 6901.

Symphony No. 5. Toscanini and NBC Symphony: Victor LM-1757 and 6901.

Symphony No. 6 (*Pastorale*). Toscanini and NBC Symphony: Victor LM-1755 and 6901.

Symphony No. 9. Toscanini and NBC Symphony: Victor LM-6009 and 6901.

Quartet Op. 59 No. 3. Budapest Quartet: Columbia ML-4581.

Quartet Op. 130. Budapest Quartet: Columbia ML-4584.

Quartet Op. 132. Budapest Quartet: Columbia ML-4586.

BERLIOZ

La Damnation de Faust: Danse des Sylphes and *Menuet des Feux-Follets.* Van Otterloo and Lamoureux Orchestra: Epic LC-3054. Cluytens and Paris Opera Orchestra: Angel 35431.

Roméo et Juliette: La Reine Mab. Toscanini and NBC Symphony: Victor LM-6026. Cluytens and Paris Opera Orchestra: Angel 35431.

BRAHMS

Variations on a Theme of Haydn. Toscanini and NBC Symphony: Victor LM-1725.

DEBUSSY

Nuages. Cantelli and Philharmonia Orchestra: Angel 35525.

La Mer. Watch for the release here of Cantelli's per-

formance on HMV ALP-1228. Toscanini and NBC
Symphony: Victor LM-1833.

Ibéria.   Toscanini and NBC Symphony: Victor LM-
1833. Argenta and Orchestre de la Suisse Ro-
mande: London LL-1735 (mono) and CS-6013
(stereo).

HAYDN

t **Symphony No. 104.** Von Karajan and Vienna Philharmonic: Victor LD (mono) and LDS (stereo)
2347. Beecham and Royal Philharmonic: Capitol
GCR (mono) and SGCR (stereo) 7198.

t **Quartet Op. 54 No. 1.** Amadeus Quartet: Angel
45024.

Quartet Op. 74 No. 2. Griller Quartet: Vanguard
VRS-1042 (mono) and VSD-2034 (stereo).

MOZART

t **Symphony in G minor** (K.550). Toscanini and NBC
Symphony: Victor LM-1789. Von Karajan and
Vienna Philharmonic: Victor LD (mono) and
LDS (stereo) 2347.

Piano Concerto K.453. Watch for the reissue of
Edwin Fischer's pre-war performance on Angel
COLH-44.

Piano Concerto K.467. Schnabel and London Symphony under Sargent: Angel COLH-67.

Piano Concerto K.595. Schnabel and London Symphony under Barbirolli: Angel COLH-67.

t **Piano Concerto K.466.** Watch for the reissue of the
post-war Schnabel performance formerly on Victor LHMV-1012. Edwin Fischer and Philharmonia
Orchestra: Angel 35593.

Music for the man who enjoys Hamlet

Piano Concerto K.482. Iturbi and Paris Conservatory Concerts Orchestra: Angel 35539.

Piano Concerto K.488. Gieseking and Philharmonia Orchestra under Von Karajan: Columbia ML-4536.

Piano Concerto K.491. Watch for the reissue of the post-war Schnabel performance formerly on Victor LHMV-1012. Watch for the reissue of Edwin Fischer's pre-war performance on Angel COLH-44. Gieseking and Philharmonia Orchestra under Von Karajan: Angel 35501.

Piano Concerto K.271. Myra Hess and Perpignan Festival Orchestra under Casals: Columbia ML-4568.

Violin Concerto K.219. Grumiaux and Vienna Symphony under Paumgartner: Epic LC-3157.

Quartet K.458 (*Hunt*). Budapest Quartet: Columbia ML-4727.

Quintet in G minor (K.516). Budapest Quartet and Trampler: Columbia ML-5192.

Quintet K.515. Budapest Quartet and Trampler: Columbia ML-5192.

Le Nozze de Figaro. Performance conducted by Leinsdorf: Victor LM (mono) and LSC (stereo) 6408. Performance conducted by Böhm: Epic SC-6022.

Don Giovanni: Catalogue Aria. Corena: London 5194.

MUSORGSKY

Boris Godunov: Ah, I am suffocating. Chaliapin: Angel COLH-100.

145

SCHUBERT

Sonata in B flat major.   Schnabel. Angel COLH-33.

• Symphony No. 9.   Toscanini and NBC Symphony:
   Victor LM-1835.

• Quintet Op. 163.   Budapest Quartet and B. Heifetz:
   Columbia ML-4437. Stern, Schneider, Katims,
   Casals and Tortelier: Columbia ML-4714.

Gretchen am Spinnrade.   Elisabeth Schwarzkopf and
   Edwin Fischer: Angel 35022.

TCHAIKOVSKY

Symphony No. 6 (*Pathétique*).   Watch for the release
   here of the Cantelli performance on HMV ALP-
   1042 and formerly on Victor LHMV-1047. Stein-
   berg and Pittsburgh Symphony: Capitol P-8272.
   Toscanini and NBC Symphony: Victor LM-1036.

VERDI

Aida: O patria mia.   Leonie Rysanek: Victor LM-
   2262.

La Traviata: Ah! fors' è lui.   Maria Callas: Cetra
   50167.

La Traviata: Prelude to Act 3.   In performance of
   opera conducted by Toscanini: Victor LM-6003.

WAGNER

Die Meistersinger: Prelude to Act 3.   Toscanini and
   NBC Symphony: Victor LM-6020.

Die Meistersinger: Quintet.   In performance of opera
   conducted by Kempe: Angel 3572.

Tristan und Isolde: Prelude to Act 3.   In performance
   of opera conducted by Furtwängler: Angel 3588.

INDEX TO THE MUSIC

INDEX TO SUBJECTS

ACKNOWLEDGMENTS

I am deeply indebted to Roger Dakin for his comments, criticisms and suggestions at every step in the planning and writing of the book.

The New York Music Library (58th Street) allowed me to borrow a rare musical score that I needed.

The following permissions were given me to quote passages of music:

Debussy: *La Mer*. Copyright 1905. Permission granted by Durand & Cie, Paris, and Elkan-Vogel Co., Inc., Philadelphia, copyright owners.

Debussy: *Nuages*. Permission granted by Jean Jobert, Paris, and Elkan-Vogel Co., Inc., Philadelphia.

The introductory section was published in advance of the rest of the book in *The American Scholar*.